The Positive Enneagram

A New Approach
to the Nine Personality Types

The title of Susan Rhodes' book on the enneagram neatly sums up her thesis: that the enneagram is best viewed as a *positive* system of personal transformation, and that this view is something new in the enneagram field. The author brings new direction and insights to the study and use of this compelling means of inner development. In so doing, she points out the limitations of describing human personality as negative and fixated and develops instead a model emphasizing its positive and dynamic aspects. Thus, "process" trumps "stuckness."

Making her case in a clear and engaging style, the author argues that personality type is innate, discusses the enneagram from a quantum perspective, and explains the open-ended nature of the system. She places the enneagram in a Gurdjieffian process context while continuing to make excellent use of it as a typology paradigm.

Rhodes' 'take' on the personality types—always a subject of great interest to students of the enneagram—demonstrates both a solid grounding in the basics and a multitude of fresh insights. These subtle and arresting elucidations of traditional teachings provide proof that the enneagram is indeed an open and evolving system.

In sum, this is a pioneering work, useful to both experienced enneagrammers and to those new to the field. My advice is to read it, learn it, and live it.

– Thomas G. Isham, author of
Dimensions of the Enneagram: Triad, Tradition, Transformation

In 1995, Andrea Isaacs and I established the *Enneagram Monthly (EM)* as a forum to discuss enneagram-related topics. At the time, there were only a handful of books on the system and few opportunities for people to exchange ideas in a public forum; even the Internet was in its infancy.

In the beginning, the *EM* featured many articles comparing the enneagram with the well-known Myers-Briggs Type Indicator (MBTI) because both systems focus on personality differences. But most authors found it difficult to compare the two, because the Jungian-based MBTI presented us with a benign view of personality while the enneagram focused more on personality as a barrier to the development of higher faculties.

After 2000, some *EM* authors suggested that we apply the emerging insights of positive psychology to our work with the enneagram. But it was not until Susan Rhodes published her landmark article, "Let's Depathologize the Enneagram!" in 2006 that the idea of a positive approach began to take tangible shape. Susan not only called for a more positive vision but explained in subsequent articles precisely how such a vision could become a reality. She explored the enneagram from a variety of perspectives, drawing from innovative work in diverse areas of inquiry: integral theory (Ken Wilber), the development of creativity (Stephen Nachmanovich), prototype theory (Eleanor Rosch), systems theory (Arthur Koestler and Margaret Wheatley), the psychology of individuation (Carl Jung), and positive psychology (Martin Seligman and others). She also discovered a way to link G. I. Gurdjieff's process enneagram with Oscar Ichazo's personality enneagram.

I was impressed with Susan's innovative ideas, analytical mind, and writing skills. In 2007, I asked her to become the first official staff writer for the *EM*. Since that time, she has published over 20 articles on the enneagram, all of them based on the premise that the nine enneagram types are positive sources of energy and information.

The Positive Enneagram presents the best of her ideas on the system in a format appealing to a wide range of readers. The book opens new doors for enneagram explorations and shows us that the enneagram is a system for identifying not just our blind spots, but our possibilities and potentials.

— Jack Labanauskas, publisher of the *Enneagram Monthly*

The Positive Enneagram

A New Approach
to the Nine Personality Types

Susan Rhodes

Acknowledgments: Many thanks to the friends who inspired me to write this book, who read early drafts, and who otherwise assisted in its publication, editing, and distribution, including Deborah DiMichele, Claudio Garibaldi, Dina Innominato, Ed Morler, Pamela Silimperi, Mary Solomon, Laurie Tucker, Elizabeth Wagele, Rachel Whalley, Judy Windt, Sheela Word, Chiri Word, and Tilotoma Word; many thanks to Charmaine Sungy for sharing her enneagram insights, especially on the energetic qualities of the types. Thanks to the Thompson family—Norm, Adél, Hanna, and Norman—for adopting me into their home, thus helping me stay sane during the writing of this book. Special thanks to Jack Labanauskas and SueAnn McKean for their ongoing support and inspiration.

First printing: July 2009
Second printing: August 2009

All content, photos & graphics by Susan Rhodes unless otherwise noted; back cover photo by Seth Wonner (www.sethwonner.com).

ISBN 978-0-9824792-0-9

You can order this book at Amazon.com.
For quantity discounts, please contact the author at:

Geranium Press
12345 Lake City Way NE #280
Seattle, WA 98125
geraniumpress@gmail.com

GERANIUM PRESS

To Hanna & Norman
little friends who taught me big things

Contents

Introduction

For several years, I've been the staff writer for the longest-running periodical published on the enneagram, the *Enneagram Monthly*. So every month, I have to think about something to write. This has given me the opportunity to deeply reflect on the nature of the enneagram and the nine enneagram types.

The enneagram is a wonderful system with many applications, among them the description of human individuality. It delineates nine enneagram types, each of which has a unique core motivation unlike that of the other eight types. In addition to describing the types, it also describes the interactions among them. So it's a powerful tool for understanding ourselves and improving our relationships.

However, the main focus of most enneagram books is not on the gifts of each type, but on its limitations or distortions. This is because, while the enneagram types are described as personality types, the term *personality* is not used to refer to individual differences in temperament. It is instead used to describe character disorders or psychological fixations. So the nine enneagram types are not just personality types—they are *fixated* personality types. In fact, from this perspective, personality is basically fixated in nature.

This idea always seemed strange to me. When I looked at the enneagram, I saw the nine enneagram types as nine different kinds of people. I had already studied the Myers-Briggs Type Indicator (MBTI), a Jungian-based personality profiling system, and was really impressed with it. It gave me a great deal of insight into my own temperament and that of other people.

I became interested in looking for systems that might describe individuality in other ways. I ran into several, but they were all relatively limited in scope. It wasn't until I found the enneagram that I knew I had a system that could rival the MBTI.

In fact, I soon saw that the enneagram was actually a much deeper, more elemental system than the MBTI. It had the power not only to delineate behavioral differences but to describe the nine core motivations behind them. It also described the relationship of each type to the other eight types. The more I studied the system, the more compelling I found it.

There was only one problem: the pessimistic tone of the type descriptions. Instead of just being personality profiles, most of them sounded like neurosis profiles, even when the authors tried to put a positive spin on the descriptions. I didn't understand why.

It took me years to figure out the answer. What I discovered is that when the teachings on the enneagram were first disseminated 30 or 40 years ago, they were presented as part of a broader philosophy of life—a philosophy that assumes that ordinary people are basically lost, deluded, or asleep. Psychologically, this means that most of us are neurotic (or worse).

We can see this pattern in Claudio Naranjo's influential book, *Character and Neurosis*, where the author links each of the nine enneagram types to a major category of mental illness. His negative view of the types seems to have been inherited from his own teacher, Oscar Ichazo, who originated the practice of using the enneagram as a means of delineating differences in motivation. However, Ichazo believed that people differ not just in motivation but in *fixated* motivation. So he actually called his best-known enneagram the Enneagram of Fixations, based on the idea that there are nine different ways in which people get trapped in patterns of compulsive thinking.

This idea seems to have its roots in the Freudian notion that adult neuroses are the result of getting stuck (fixated) at an early stage of childhood development due to some sort of trauma. Fixation is what supposedly lies at the root of mental disturbance in adults. What is interesting, however, is that in the teachings on the enneagram, this stuckness is assumed to be universal: we *all* get fixated, which is why we all have an enneagram (fixation) type.

This idea is often expressed in more spiritualized language as the hypothesis that ego obscures Essence. The argument goes as follows:

We are born in Essence—in a state of Oneness with the essential self. But we inevitably lose this Oneness as the result of wounds received in infancy and early childhood. The result is the development of a false (ego) self whose nature is determined by the kind of wound we experienced. The enneagram is said to show us the nine kinds of false selves that develop as a result, each of which is associated with a cognitive fixation, an emotional passion or sin, and a psychological defense mechanism designed to bolster the false ego.

This notion has a certain romantic appeal, and is the basis for a "back to Eden" mentality which has been the hallmark of romantics for at least two centuries. The language of the argument varies, but the basic theme is always the same: that each of us used to be in touch with something wonderful with which we lost contact (usually because of gaining knowledge, rationality, or individuality) and which can be restored only if we can somehow return to this idyllic state.

There's only one problem—it doesn't work. Returning to an earlier stage in development doesn't restore people to paradise, it just restores them to a state of dependency. This is assuming that we could actually pull this off, which is doubtful.

I base my enneagram work on a different premise: the idea that we don't have to divest ourselves of personality, individuality, or ego in order to experience Essence. Individuality does not block Essence; it coexists with Essence. We have both an eternal (essential) self that does not change and an ever-evolving and highly idiosyncratic self which does change. These two selves are not really separate; they're just different aspects of the same self.

While I see some benefit in being aware of shortcomings or blind spots, I see little benefit in dwelling on them. I also don't believe that the effects of early conditioning are mainly traumatic. Conditioning can be either positive or negative, and most of us get some mix of the two. Even the wounds created by aversive conditioning are not sufficient to actually determine the basic structure of our personality—or to create a personality that is entirely false.

I see the basic structure of our personality as innate. It exists as a blueprint that is with us at birth and which gradually unfolds from that point on. What determines the nature of the blueprint is a mystery, but it has something to do with our soul's purpose in life.

Our enneagram type is foundational to this blueprint, because it gives us the core motivation around which our personality is organized. No matter what our conditioning, it can't change the basic matrix of the personality. That's why our enneagram type is with us for life.

What *can* be affected by conditioning is the coherence and balance of the personality. Children in a stable home with loving parents tend to have more coherent, balanced personalities than those in less stable (or even abusive) situations. All the same, it's easy to overestimate the effects of unhealthy conditioning and underestimate the effects of healthy conditioning, in part because Freudian psychology has so permeated our beliefs about childhood. The idea that we're permanent victims of our early conditioning (whose effects can be mitigated but never really healed) is as pervasive as it is pernicious.

The more we dwell on this idea, the more we condition ourselves to feel trapped and discouraged. We become "fixated on the fixation." And this kind of obsession leads down a dead-end road.

We don't have to see ourselves this way. In the end, it's a choice—it's not something inevitable. We make choices throughout our lives, and each choice has consequences, good or bad. The idea is to learn from those choices, so we can make better choices next time. So the idea of "thinking positive" is not about ignoring life's challenges or reframing them to avoid taking responsibility—it's about acknowledging them, learning from them, and *then moving on*.

The Sufis have a saying: "First remember your faults, then forget them." To become aware of our shortcomings is good, but to belabor them is not. Once we acknowledge our weaknesses, it's time to reconsider our actions in light of this new knowledge.

This can be a painful process, because it means seeing ourselves as we actually are. It means reflecting on our acts, on our intentions, and on our lives—taking everything out of the closet to see what's there. And then putting it back again in better order. It also entails a decision to take responsibility for our future acts (which can be even more painful!). But it's what paves the way for something better—for peace, for healing, and for what Buddhists call "right action."

So focusing on our faults (or on our wounds) is something we do for a brief period only. If we do it for too long, it becomes counterproductive. Instead of helping us move beyond wrong-headed attitudes and behaviors, it actually reinforces them. We become stuck in the past, endlessly hashing over past difficulties and mistakes. We limit ourselves and come to project that limitation on everything we see.

When we encounter something new, like the enneagram, it becomes just another vehicle for reinforcing our negative habits of mind. We don't see the enneagram as it actually is—we see it through the lens of our own negativity. So instead of a system that shows us how to free ourselves from self-negating patterns, it becomes a system for trapping us within them.

When G. I. Gurdjieff originally taught the enneagram in the early 20th century, he did not portray it as a system for demonstrating the nature of human limitation but as a system that revealed life's vitality. As he observed, "A motionless enneagram is a dead symbol; the living symbol is in motion."* That is why Gurdjieff's process model of the enneagram retains a tremendous vitality and power. But when the enneagram was later used to describe the nine archetypal ways that people differ, those who initially worked with it did so using a model of human nature that was not dynamic, but fixed. It emphasized human limitation rather than human potential.

This is the model that we have all inherited. It's a powerful model, because it reveals the nine types of core motivation possible for a human being. That's why it has such great explanatory power. At the same time, it assumes that these core motivations arise not from the self, but from a false (conditioned) ego. From this viewpoint, when we study the nine types, we're not studying nine types of people—we're studying nine types of false selves.

While I see the value of understanding the typical challenges faced by each type, I don't see the value of making them a defining feature of the type. If the enneagram were really a system designed

---

*See P. D. Ouspensky's *In Search of the Miraculous,* Harcourt: 1949/2001, p. 294.

to describe fixation, its geometry would reflect that distortion, which it does not. When we look at the enneagram, what we see is a figure of great power and beauty: a circle (symbolizing oneness), nine points (symbolizing nine aspects of that oneness), and nine inner connecting lines (symbolizing our inherent interconnectedness). Alternatively, we can see the circle as the human psyche, the points as different aspects of the psyche, and the lines as the relationships between different parts of ourselves (and between all the parts and the whole).

There is nothing in the geometry that shows us a distorted view of human consciousness—in fact, just the opposite is true. The figure visually reflects the idea that *no individual is cut off from Essence*— nor are we cut off from each other. The illusion of separation is just that: an illusion. It is not reality.

Understanding this point will change the way we work with the enneagram. Why? Because it will enable us to see why it's impossible to think of the enneagram solely as a system for describing human deficiency. As Jung has sensibly pointed out, we heal the psyche not by villainizing its shadow aspects (rejecting them as false) but by claiming and integrating them (a process he called *individuation*). It is via individuation that we become more differentiated (more of an individual).

The enneagram can show us the key principle around which that individuality is organized: our core motivation. That's where individuality originates. Each of the nine types embodies a particular kind of individuality, fueled by a particular kind of motivational energy.

When we study the enneagram, we learn how this energy works—how it can be both applied and misapplied. Once we realize the dynamics of each type, we can use this understanding to make better decisions in our lives.

But no matter how good we get, we're never going to have a perfect personality. We're never going to become the kind of people who never make mistakes, because life is too dynamic for that. The moment is always rushing at us, sometimes a little quicker than we can manage. So sometimes we're in synch and sometimes we're not.

Fortunately, the personality does not have to be perfect—it just has to be *functional*.

So my approach in working with the enneagram is to assume an essentially optimistic view of both the enneagram and the nine types. I realize that the energy of the types can be misused, but that is part of our learning process. If we pounce on every mistake—seeing it as evidence of our "false self"—we deprive ourselves of the opportunity to learn and grow.

Enneagram Types as a Guide to Living

It's the type energy that fuels our ability to learn and grow. This energy is a highly dynamic, energizing force, like light, that is primordial in nature and with us at birth. This is why type is more like a temperament type than a personality type.

From a spiritual viewpoint, our enneagram type is closely associated with our soul nature and the purpose of the soul's incarnation. This is why it has a lot to tell us about our *dharma* or life path. More to the point, it has a lot to tell us about which life paths are *not* compatible with our inner nature.

Although some people seem to be blessed with the intuition necessary to figure this out on their own, many of us are not. Too many us of spend years in our youth wandering through life, trying things out that don't work for us simply because we don't know ourselves well enough to make a better choice. While a certain amount of trial and error is unavoidable, too much can leave us feeling like we're going through life playing a perpetual game of Blind Man's Bluff.

The enneagram can help us avoid bumping into previously invisible obstacles. It doesn't eliminate them, but it can help us see where they are and how they're likely to trip us up. The enneagram can help people answer some really basic questions about life:

- Why am I here?
- What work can I do?
- How can I have better relationships?
- How can I live my life in a way that is really fulfilling?

The Positive Enneagram introduces a way of working with the enneagram that helps people answer questions like these. While it covers many of the same topics as other books on the enneagram, the subtext is very different—because underlying every word is the assumption that type is a positive force in our lives, rather than an albatross around our necks.

Organization

The book has nine chapters and three appendixes. While many enneagram books organize their chapters by the enneagram types (with one chapter per type), I organized this book in a way that would emphasize different ways of looking at the types.

There's an overview of the entire book (Chapter 1), followed by a description of all nine types (Chapter 2). Chapters 3 – 7 present more detailed descriptions of the types: as energy types (Chapter 3), connecting points (Chapter 4), subtypes (Chapters 5 and 6), and wing types (Chapter 7).

Chapter 8 links Ichazo's personality enneagram to Gurdjieff's process enneagram (thereby demonstrating the dynamic nature of the nine types). And Chapter 9 presents a framework for working with the enneagram in a new way: as a living system designed to help us transcend dualistic thinking, find direction in life, and develop our creativity.

There are also three appendixes designed to help you determine your enneagram type and subtype. There are two tests for discovering your type (a qualitative/narrative test with brief descriptions of each type in Appendix A and an 180-statement quantitative test in Appendix B) and one for determining your subtype arena (Appendix C).

While the tests can be helpful for determining your type, they're not really a substitute for self-reflection. Without reflection, knowing your type doesn't mean all that much. It just becomes another interesting fact to file away and forget.

Readers with prior knowledge of the enneagram are bound to notice that in order to discuss the enneagram from a positive point of view, I found it necessary to modify some aspects of enneagram theory that would otherwise be inconsistent with a positive interpretation of the types. These differences are particularly evident in the chapters on the energy centers (Chapter 3), the subtype arenas (Chapter 5), and the enneagram as a living system (Chapter 9).

I also introduce new ideas that complement existing teachings: the idea of treating the subtype arenas separately from the enneagram types (Chapter 5) and of linking the personality and process enneagrams (Chapter 8).

The result is a book designed to appeal both to people who have never heard of the enneagram and those with extensive experience working with the system.

A Positive Outlook

I originally wanted to write a book that would simply introduce the enneagram to people who would respond to a more positive portrayal of the types. I wasn't planning to talk about why I presented the material from an optimistic standpoint. But I soon realized that because of the existing body of work on the enneagram, I had to explain why this book is different from other enneagram books. Otherwise, people might find the presentation confusing. That's why I include an extended explanation in this introduction. It's also in the first chapter of the book in an abbreviated form.

The ideas expressed in this book are based on my personal experiences and impressions from working with the enneagram. I'm not claiming that I've discovered the truth about the enneagram—this is something that we each have to discover for ourselves. My goal here is simply to share a way of working with the system that I've found to be both practical and inspiring.

I remain grateful to the enneagram pioneers who originally developed, interpreted, and disseminated the teachings on the enneagram to the public at large, despite my goal in this book of reinterpreting some aspects of those teachings. Without this early work, the field would lack the solid foundation upon which others can build. I support all efforts to inform people about this wonderful system, which I see as immensely valuable for humankind.

— Susan Rhodes, July 2009

Enneagram Overview

The enneagram is a universal system with many applications. It has a number of unique features, one of which is its association with this intriguing-looking geometric figure:

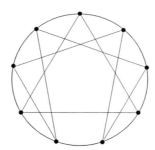

This figure is not just symbolic of the enneagram, it actually *is* the enneagram. This means that the enneagram system is not just a mental construct made up by a person—it's an independent system based on precise geometric relationships involving the circle, its nine points, and various connecting lines. So once we have a basic grasp of how the system works, we can explore it for ourselves, using its geometry as a guide.

When we look more closely, what we see is a circle with nine points that are equidistant (40° apart). The points (called *enneagram types* or *points of view*) are connected by an interesting series of lines that are symmetrical vertically although not horizontally. There are many other interesting characteristics of the geometry, but the three essential features are the *circle*, the *points*, and the *lines*.

The Circle, the Points, and the Lines

The geometry of the enneagram has a profound meaning. It serves as a symbolic reminder about the nature of life and life processes. The circle represents *wholeness*, the points represent the *nine different ways* in which life can manifest, and the lines, the *energetic ties* that connect the parts with the whole.

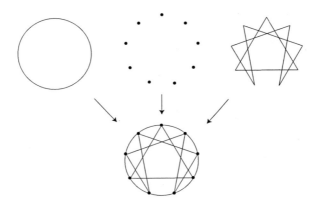

If we just look at the inner lines themselves, we can also break them up to create two other figures: the *triangle* and the *hexad*.

There's also an *energy flow* associated with these inner lines, as shown by the arrows on these figures:

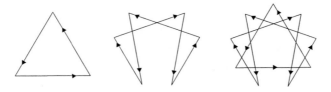

The Nine Types

Although the enneagram can be used for multiple purposes, it's most often used today as a system for distinguishing nine different patterns of motivation that give rise to nine personality types. Each point on the enneagram circle represents one of the types.

However, I see the nine points as representing something more basic than personality—something more like innate temperament or disposition. So I prefer to think of the types as *energy types, motivation types,* or *individuality types.* But for simplicity's sake, I refer to the enneagram the same way as everybody else does: as the *personality enneagram.*

Each of the types can be described in many ways, depending on our purpose. However, the most basic way of describing the types is simply with a number—a number associated with one of the nine points on the enneagram circle:

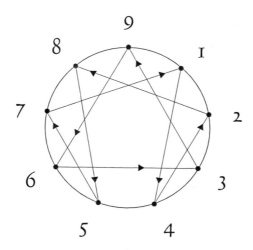

Referring to the nine types by number gives us an objective way to talk about each type, whatever label we use to describe it. Type One is always Type One, but Type One can also be called the Pioneer, Definer, Lawmaker, Judge, Crusader, Detailer, etc., depending on the context for our discussion. We'll look at a variety of these contexts in order to explore different dimensions of the types.

The chart below provides the first of many descriptions of the types. You'll notice that each time I describe the type, I usually do it a little differently, from a slightly different angle. So although we have here just one label per type (to keep things simple at the start), at the end we wind up with many labels, each of which reflects a different facet of the same energy.

Chapter 2 introduces the types in more depth; subsequent chapters break them down into wing types, subtypes, and points in a process.

The Nine Types

1 **THE PERFECTER**	careful, conscientious, serious, single pointed, idealizing, values-oriented
2 **THE PEOPLE PERSON**	supportive, involved, concerned, committed, interactive, people-oriented
3 **THE SELF-TESTER**	busy, practical, Type A, aspiring, competitive, adaptive, task-oriented
4 **THE DEEP SEA DIVER**	sensitive, aesthetic, intense, deep, creative, original, meaning-oriented
5 **THE PUZZLE-SOLVER**	shy, detached, ingenious, reflective, private, innovative, knowledge-oriented
6 **THE STEWARD**	cautious, ambivalent, skeptical, sensing, anxious, equivocating, safety-oriented
7 **THE IMPROVISER**	curious, fun-loving, restless, shifting, entrepreneurial, stimulation-oriented
8 **THE MASTER**	strong, assured, masterful, grounded, frank, magnetic, power-oriented
9 **THE STORYTELLER**	kind, unassuming, imaginative, open, accepting, fair, nature-oriented

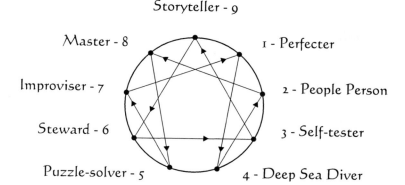

Storyteller - 9

Master - 8

Improviser - 7

Steward - 6

Puzzle-solver - 5

1 - Perfecter

2 - People Person

3 - Self-tester

4 - Deep Sea Diver

The Nine Types on the Enneagram

My Take on the Types

There are three key assumptions I make when talking about the nine enneagram types:

1. type is with us for life (we never switch types)
2. type is innate (with us from birth)
3. type is a source of positive motivation

The first of these assumptions—that type is with us for life—is based on traditional teachings on the enneagram. The second and third are not.

Type is often said to be the product of early childhood conditioning. But it makes more sense to consider it innate. For one thing, our type never changes; if we start out as Type 3, we stay Type 3 for life. For that reason alone, it would make sense to assume that type is innate, that it is mysteriously hard-wired into our circuitry. Otherwise, it could potentially change. But a more telling reason is that research on infant cognition and perception overwhelmingly supports the idea that individuality is present from birth.

When the enneagram teachings were first disseminated in the 1970s, this research was not yet conclusive and the influence of both behaviorism (which held that infants were blank slates) and Freudian theory (which characterized young infants as completely self-absorbed) was still strong. So that's why the enneagram types were assumed to be the product of conditioning, which was assumed from a Freudian viewpoint to have a more or less detrimental effect on the developing infant. As a result, the personality that emerged in early childhood was almost sure to be deficient in some way.

Little effort was made to subject these ideas to serious empirical scrutiny. But they nevertheless became influential. As a result, those who originally developed and taught the personality enneagram were considerably influenced by them. Viewing personality as basically the same thing as an enneagram type, they attributed to *type* an essentially negative character. Type became viewed as a false self that was said to obscure our original state of essential being. The nine types were said to represent nine ways that the self becomes fixated, compulsive, and unbalanced.

Because everyone who learned the enneagram received more or less the same teaching, this view of the types as distorted versions of the self became widespread. However, the basic assumptions of this view have been increasingly undercut by scientific research, especially research on genetics and infant development. This research shows that many psychological attributes that we once saw as the effects of social conditioning and maladjustment are actually innate, including the basic structures of the personality. That's why it becomes hard to avoid the conclusion that the basic structures of personality (and therefore enneagram type) are present at birth, not acquired later on.

If we throw out the idea that type is a form of conditioning, we can also throw out the idea that type is inherently neurotic, disturbed, or fixated. If type exists from birth (at least in nascent form), then it cannot be defined as disturbed unless we want to make the claim that human nature is inherently unbalanced. And I'm not willing to make that claim.

That's why I developed an alternative approach for discussing the enneagram and the nine types—an approach based on a more positive assessment of human personality and potential.

The Three Energy Centers

One of the easiest ways to get acquainted with the types is by looking at the kind of energy associated with them. While each type has its own distinctive energy, the type energy arises out of one of three energy centers: the Body Center, Heart Center, or Head Center.

- **Body Center** (Types 8-9-1). The energy of the body center is fiery and quick to ignite (or explode), but also quick to cool. It is instinctual or sensate in nature (attuned to nature and natural processes).

- **Heart Center** (Types 2-3-4). The energy of the heart center is watery and flowing. It spreads out and seeps downward, unless it is contained within a vessel. Because it is heavy and fluid, it requires stimulation in order to circulate.

- **Head Center** (Types 5-6-7). The energy of the head center is airy, cool, and light. It moves upward and is hard to contain but easy to agitate, like the air. It is invisible but pervasive.

We each have the energy of all three centers within us. At the same time, depending on our enneagram type, one of these energies will predominate, influencing us more than the other two; see Chapter 3 for more.

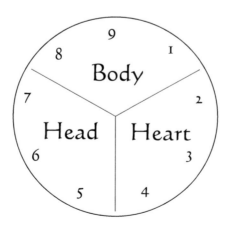

The Three Energy Centers

Connecting Points

Each enneagram point of view is connected to two other points via the inner lines on the circle. These connecting points are of special significance, because they represent two additional sources of energy that support the energy of our type. The charts below and opposite give a brief introduction to the connecting points for each point of view.

The nature of the connection can also depend on whether we're moving *with* the arrows or *against* the arrows describing the flow of energy on the inner lines. Moving with the arrows takes us to our *stress point* (the place we access when we need more support); moving against them takes us to our *security point* (the place we access when we're feeling more confident and outgoing). See the charts on this page and the next for a brief summary of how the two connecting points relate to the point with which they connect; see Chapter 4 for more. (Note: the top descriptions refer to the stress points; the bottom descriptions refer to the security points.)

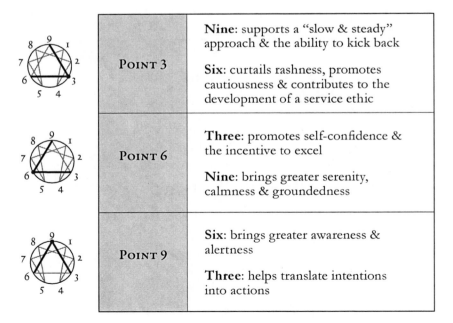

	Point 3	**Nine:** supports a "slow & steady" approach & the ability to kick back **Six:** curtails rashness, promotes cautiousness & contributes to the development of a service ethic
	Point 6	**Three:** promotes self-confidence & the incentive to excel **Nine:** brings greater serenity, calmness & groundedness
	Point 9	**Six:** brings greater awareness & alertness **Three:** helps translate intentions into actions

	POINT 1	**Four:** allows judgment to be informed by deep conviction **Seven:** brings spontaneity, enthusiasm & the ability to lighten up
	POINT 2	**Eight:** helps develop assertiveness & self-confidence **Four:** supports the deepening of surface emotions & a sense of genuineness
	POINT 4	**Two:** provides the incentive to cooperate & connect with others **One:** enhances self-discipline, self-reliance & the ability to behave appropriately

	POINT 5	**Seven:** brings a playful curiosity, ingenuity & the ability to see connections **Eight:** enhances groundedness, assertiveness & the ability to act
	POINT 7	**One:** supports the development of precision & care **Five:** brings the ability to slow down, reflect & be still
	POINT 8	**Five:** promotes greater sensitivity & a sense of interiority **Two:** supports the development of heartfulness & good will

Enneagram Subtypes

Studying the wing types gives us a way to make finer-grained distinctions when considering within-type differences. Another way to break down the type is by looking at how different people of the same type seek fulfillment in life.

Some people are *extremely independent.* They enjoy doing things on their own and like their own space. Others are *intensity-seekers* who are inspired by the thrill of romance, the fascination of the deep, or the dizzying heights of spiritual transcendence. Yet others are focused on *social relations;* they are at their best when participating in group activities like social galas, community work, or political activism.

In the language of the enneagram world, the independent folks are *self-preservation subtypes,* the intensity-seekers are *sexual subtypes,* and the participatory types are *social subtypes.* The subtype approach allows us to determine our type and then to refine our understanding of the type by seeing how its energy shows up in one of these three subtype arenas:

- Arena of the **self** (focus on ONE = self-preservation subtype)
  (selfhood, individuality, survival, responsibility, ethics, independence)

- Arena of **intimacy** (focus on TWO = sexual subtype)
  (love, intimacy, passion, creativity, the Shadow, mysticism, the Beloved)

- Arena of **social relations** (focus on THREE OR MORE = social subtype)
  (group dynamics, community, diplomacy, politics, social awareness, status)

I call these three areas of focus *arenas* because they are like spheres of activity in which events take place. Put them together, and you have a three-ring circus—just like in life!

Each of us participates in all three arenas, usually on a daily basis. We take care of our personal needs, seek creative or intimate fulfillment, and play various roles as members of our community and society. But for most people, one of these arenas tends to be dominant. This is the arena that determines our enneagram subtype.

The power of the three-arena subtype system becomes apparent when we combine it with the nine-category enneagram system.

We can then generate a matrix of 27 **subtype profiles** that are quite detailed in nature. The chart below provides labels for each of these profiles; the graphic on the next page shows how they can be mapped onto the enneagram.

Enneagram Subtypes

POINT ▼	**SELF-PRESERVATION ARENA** *(focus is on the self, bodily integrity & the home)*	**SEXUAL ARENA** *(focus is on intimacy, creativity, aspiration & intensity)*	**SOCIAL ARENA** *(focus is on the group, community & society)*
1	Detailer	Crusader	Lawmaker
2	Matriarch	Romantic	Diplomat
3	Pragmatist	Superstar	Politician
4	Artisan	Dramatist	Social Critic
5	Archivist	Wizard	Professor
6	Family Preserver	Scrapper	Guardian
7	Bon Vivant	Trickster	Visionary
8	Weight Lifter	Knight	Leader
9	Comfort Seeker	Mystic	Cooperator

On the enneagram below,

- the **self-preservation subtypes** are on the *inner circle*
- the **sexual subtypes** are on the *middle circle*
- the **social subtypes** are on the *outer circle*

Although it takes a certain amount of time to really absorb the differences between the 27 subtype categories, it's well worth the effort, because it really brings the enneagram system to life. Also, people who have trouble initially typing themselves sometimes find that they can recognize themselves more easily by looking at subtype (rather than type) profiles. See Chapters 5 and 6 for details.

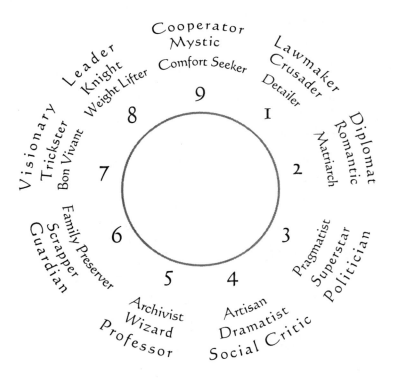

The 27 Subtypes

Wing Types

Each of the enneagram types has a neighbor on either side. These are its *wings*. Usually, one of those wings will exert a stronger influence than the other. As a result, it's possible to break each type into two halves, depending on which wing dominates. So if a person is a Three, he's probably a hard worker. But if he has a strong Two wing, he's probably more attracted to working with other people; if he has a strong Four wing, he's probably more attracted to working independently.

The 18 wing types are mapped onto the enneagram below and also listed in the chart on the following page. See Chapter 7 for more.

The 18 Wing Types

Enneagram Wing Types

1w9	THE DEFINER	reserved, quiet, detailed, devoted, irritable
1w2	THE REFORMER	impassioned, adamant, determined, convicted
2w1	THE SOCIAL WORKER	concerned, engaged, sympathetic, encouraging
2w3	THE SOCIALIZER	gracious, engaging, inviting, sociable, eager
3w2	THE MANAGER	adaptable, organized, clever, pleasant, polished
3w4	THE PROFESSIONAL	business-like, ambitious, focused, independent
4w3	THE SPECIALIST	individualistic, distinctive, in style, high-powered
4w5	THE ARTISTE	deep, intense, moody, disciplined, focused
5w4	THE ICONOCLAST	unconventional, offbeat, shamanic, penetrating
5w6	THE THINKER	dry, intellectual, proficient, self-contained
6w5	THE SERVER	thoughtful, conscientious, attentive, retrospective
6w7	THE WIT	jumpy, self-conscious, witty, winsome, respectful
7w6	THE COMEDIAN	funny, edgy, fun, high-spirited, playful, restless
7w8	THE ADVENTURER	adventurous, energetic, fast-moving, high-energy
8w7	THE POWER BROKER	confident, blunt, forward-moving, unrepentant
8w9	THE POWERHOUSE	grounded, solid, massive, deliberate, forceful
9w8	THE MOUNTAIN	steady, patient, absorbing, waiting, observant
9w1	THE ANTICIPATOR	open, childlike, idealizing, starry-eyed, impatient

The Types as Stages of Transformation

So far we've looked at the basic geometry of the enneagram, its three energy centers, its 18 wing types, its 27 subtypes, and its connecting points. My intent is not to overwhelm but to provide an overview of the system—we'll return to each of these topics in later chapters.

But you might notice that I don't just talk about the types and their variants, but try to map them directly onto the enneagram whenever possible. This is because seeing them on the enneagram helps us understand the underlying properties of each point of view. We notice things we wouldn't notice if we were just reading a list of type attributes.

We see, for example, how the types are connected with one another—some by being next to other types on the circle, some by the inner lines, and some seemingly not at all. (Actually, if you look hard enough, you discover that all the types are connected. It's just that some connections are more obvious or direct than others.)

One of the most useful things that we can notice when we look at the enneagram is the relationship between adjacent types. We've already looked at this in the discussion on wing types, but we can use the information on wings to look not only at how wings relate to types but at how *all* the types relate to one another in a progressive flow—how Type 1 shifts to Type 2, Type 2 to Type 3, etc.

The fact that each type can be seen to shift into the next is not just an interesting artifact. It reflects a profound truth, which is that each enneagram point of view is not just an arbitrary set of characteristics existing in isolation. It is part of a larger context—a context that is both meaningful and highly dynamic.

There is actually an energy that flows between the types following the outside path of the circle—an energy flow that links all the types together. They are all part of a larger process, a process that describes how a new idea arises, is developed, and is brought to completion as a finished product.

The idea of the enneagram as a process started with G. I. Gurdjieff, who hinted that the enneagram was actually a sort of perpetual motion machine, with energy flowing around the edge of the circle and also along the inner lines. Later, Arica founder Oscar Ichazo envisioned the enneagram in quite a different way, as a system for showing nine types of personality fixation—places where energy backs up and gets stuck. But Ichazo's approach is difficult to reconcile with the idea of a dynamic process.

If we drop the idea that types are about "stuckness," then it's possible to see each type as embodying the energy associated with a particular stage in a larger process—a process that links all nine types and places them in a larger context. Here is the enneagram we know:

Now here is the enneagram as used to describe a process:

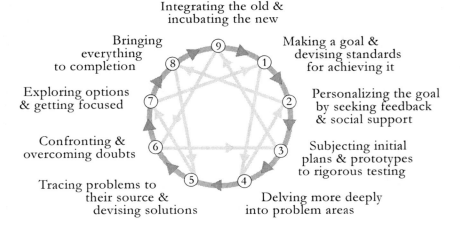

If we start at Point 1 in this process-oriented enneagram, we see how something emerges out of a period of incubation (Point 9) to become an idea or intention in need of initial development (Point 1). At Point 2, the development process begins in earnest, with the gathering of information and input from other people. At Point 3, we begin to test out our idea to see whether it has enough merit to proceed. Assuming the answer is yes, we proceed to reflect more deeply on all the ramifications of what we're doing (Point 4), arriving at a mental understanding of whatever problems may arise (Point 5). But this kind of understanding is not enough to overcome all problems, especially our innermost self-doubts—sometimes we need to make a leap of faith to get past our Dweller on the Threshold (Point 6). If we can make such a leap, a breakthrough is possible, leading to more options and feelings of elation (Point 7) and the need to refocus our attention to bring things to a state of completion (Point 8). Then we're ready for some R & R and time for "just being" (Point 9).

Now let's see what happens when we juxtapose the enneagram of the nine points with the process enneagram:

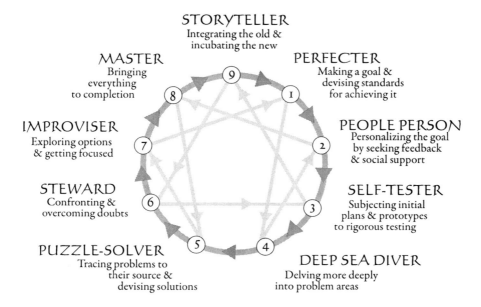

STORYTELLER
Integrating the old &
incubating the new

MASTER
Bringing
everything
to completion

PERFECTER
Making a goal &
devising standards
for achieving it

IMPROVISER
Exploring options
& getting focused

PEOPLE PERSON
Personalizing the goal
by seeking feedback
& social support

STEWARD
Confronting &
overcoming doubts

SELF-TESTER
Subjecting initial
plans & prototypes
to rigorous testing

PUZZLE-SOLVER
Tracing problems to
their source &
devising solutions

DEEP SEA DIVER
Delving more deeply
into problem areas

If we look at the labels and the process descriptions, we can see potential parallels between the enneagram type labels and the corresponding stage in a creative process, even with these very brief descriptions. The parallels are definitely there, although they may be more obvious for some enneagram types than others. Why? Because each type has many facets. So the label that works best as a type descriptor for general purposes isn't necessarily the best label for describing the type in terms of its role as a stage in a process (but see Chapter 9 for a chart listing dozens of alternative labels for each type). The chart to the right briefly describes the relationship between the types and the stages; see Chapter 8 for details.

The Enneagram as a Living System

Mapping personality to process helps us understand that we can be sitting at a stable point (like our enneagram point of view) without actually being stuck or fixated. It illustrates the fact that we don't have to think of our type as a trap—we can think of it as a source of energy, motivation, and inspiration.

The geometric form of the enneagram figure supports this way of thinking, because it directs our attention not just to nine separate types, but to the *relationships* between the types and to the *unifying orb* that encircles them. When viewed from this perspective, the enneagram is much more than a tool to identify our attributes. It's a living system. And the nine enneagram types are organs within the body of this system.

To conceive of the enneagram as a living system enables us to devise new and innovative ways to apply its teachings, for example, to break out of dualistic thinking, find direction in life, and discover how to be more in the flow of the moment (see Chapter 9).

How Type Relates to Transformation

Pt ▼	TYPE	STAGE	MAIN TASK
1	PERFECTER	Setting goals	To perfect the foundation for moving towards a goal
2	PEOPLE PERSON	Humanizing goals	To get feedback, enlist support & humanize impersonal goals
3	SELF-TESTER	Testing prototypes	To see whether our ideas are practical enough to be worth pursuing
4	DEEP SEA DIVER	Getting committed	To deepen our understanding of the project & make a commitment to continue
5	PUZZLE-SOLVER	Solving problems	To fully understand the project & solve any problems preventing its completion
6	STEWARD	Confronting doubts	To courageously overcome doubts & dutifully allow the project to evolve as it must
7	IMPROVISER	Pulling things together	To add a bit of magic & sparkle to the project just before completion
8	MASTER	Ensuring completion	To finish the process by producing something of lasting value
9	STORYTELLER	Integration & Incubation	To allow this experience to become part of our larger life story

— 2 —

Nine Types

When I have to describe the nine enneagram types, it's always hard to know what to say. This is because each type is more like an "energy signature" than a set of behaviors.

There is no one profile that fits each type to a tee. Any description we can create is at best a sketch and at worst a stereotype. Even though each type is fueled by only one kind of core motivation, there are many different ways that this motivation can show up. This is why I find the experience of watching an enneagram type panel so interesting. I always wonder, "How can the participants be so strikingly alike while at the same time so amazingly different?"

I don't know the answer to that question. But what I *do* know is that despite the fact that there are nine types, no two people of the same type are identical. There's a tremendous amount of diversity possible for each type.

So although I use one main label per type, there are many possible labels. One of the main points of this book is that type is not really a static concept, but more like a theme or process. For this reason, the type energy generates many profiles (and thus many possible labels), as we will see. But we have to start somewhere, so we'll start with the basics—and with just one main label per type.

However, if you don't see yourself in any of the nine descriptions in this chapter, don't stop here—take a look at the 27 subtypes (Chapters 5 and 6), the 18 wing types (Chapter 7), the dozens of archetypal paths associated with each type (Chapter 9), or the nine type profiles included in What's My Type – Test I (Appendix A). We all have a "home" type; we're all located somewhere on the enneagram. Finding our type is just a matter of looking at the type from the right angle.

You'll notice that the profiles in this chapter are fairly brief. This is because I'm trying to focus on only those characteristics that are really most universal about each type. More specialized traits are covered elsewhere, as indicated above.

One last comment: the type descriptions are not just descriptions of nine types of people. They are descriptions of nine foundational aspects of the individual psyche. So each type description is relevant to all of us, whether or not it is our "home" type.

Type 1: The Perfecter

Ones are usually people with definite ideas about how things ought to be. They believe in high standards, and they hold themselves (and usually others) accountable to those standards. Because they're so careful, they're often attracted to work that requires a great deal of sharp-eyed attention to small details (like precision tool-making or copy editing).

On the other hand, although they have a reputation for being neatniks, they're not inevitably neat. It's more that they like the *idea* of neatness (or at least order). But what they decide needs ordering depends upon what they value. I once had a One house mate who actually ironed his pajamas—truly a One-ish sort of preoccupation. On the other hand, he never did much of anything in the kitchen; when I moved in, I spent a week scrubbing out cabinet interiors crammed with antique jars and bric-a-brac that had accumulated due to years of house mate comings and goings. He didn't cook much and cleaned only that part of the kitchen that he used; the rest he regarded as irrelevant.

Ones can have difficulty connecting with others on an intimate level because they tend to be rather severe. Also, they value principles very highly. This doesn't always make for a warm, cuddly persona. At the same time, they make great efforts to be sincere and truthful. So they make trustworthy friends who will stand by you in a crisis.

Their fundamentally ethical perspective attracts them to organizations and systems that are values-oriented; traditionally, Ones have been very involved in religious and civic-minded organizations. They are also well-represented among political activists of all stripes.

Ones like to see things set down in black and white, and they have a limited tolerance for anything that seems fuzzy or ambiguous. They are very good at concentrating on one task at a time but can become impatient when they get interrupted or have to multi-task. They're not particularly good compromisers, because compromise goes against their instinctive tendency to define things in terms of right or wrong, good or bad. Flexibility is another ability that seldom comes naturally to Ones.

At the same time, Ones are usually quite idealistic. They're often drawn to the law as advocates, lawyers, and judges. They're frequently artistically inclined, as well; art and literature usually inspire them more than science. Most Ones like to think of themselves as logical, but what they actually mean by this is that they're careful, thorough, and disciplined. They're a "gut" type, so they actually do better when relying more on gut instinct than on analytical thinking, because the latter tends to entangle them in "A versus B" dichotomies.

Ones have a naturally fiery nature but feel a duty to restrain themselves in deference to social custom and the needs of others. But this is not an easy task. Ones tend to hold their anger inside because they don't approve of expressing it. When they hold it in too much, they eventually feel like they're going to explode. But if they "slip" and let it out, they feel ashamed. This can be a real Catch-22 situation.

But if we ever need something done right (like eye surgery or a legal contract), whom do we seek? Someone fussy and precise, like a One. That's why I enjoy having a One handyman. He's honest, hardworking, and detail-oriented; even the way he rolls up the garden hose is "just so."

Ones are often labeled Perfectionists. I instead call them Perfecters. There are two reasons for this. The first reason is that *perfectionist* has a mostly negative connotation—it's what we use to describe somebody who is overly-concerned with perfection. And while this is true of some Ones—and is one of the challenges of the type— it's not true of all Ones. Psychologically well-balanced Ones are not compulsive perfectionists; they are simply careful.

They are conscientious, too. During one enneagram workshop I attended, the on-site counselor was a One. It's easy for somebody in that role to just be available in case anybody needs help, but to otherwise relax and participate in the workshop. I noticed that this counselor was unusually attentive to what was going on, and after a particularly intensive two-day exercise, she quietly circulated among the small groups to ask us how we were doing. Until that moment, I'd never thought about it—the workshop was enthralling and I was totally immersed in it. But under her sensitive questioning, everyone in the room started to realize that we were actually like Roman candles, burning out at both ends. We needed a breather.

The counselor had intervened at just the right moment. Later, when I thought about the incident, I realized how skillfully she had done her job—not intruding but supporting us when we really needed it. It was because she was such a careful and conscientious observer.

The second reason I like to think of Ones as Perfecters is that this term captures the idea of striving to perfect an ideal in a definitive and refined manner. This is a goal that a One can really relate to.

While Ones tend to have a hard time relaxing and can have perfectionistic tendencies, they are staunch friends and responsible partners. When they learn how to unbend a little, they are also inspired speakers and receptive listeners who know how to transform dry principles into a living reality.

Type 2: The People Person

Twos are probably the most sociable people on the enneagram. They're motivated by the desire to meet people, get to know them, and develop ongoing relationships. So they tend to be extroverted and outwardly-oriented, eager to reach out to others to make friends, organize social events, and offer all manner of personal support. However, Twos don't just casually socialize—they actively engineer their relationships: they initiate them, develop them, and mold them, much more so than other types. It's through their personal relationships that they discover who they are and how they can participate in life.

Thus, most Twos work hard to cultivate some sort of social network, whether it's through their family, their workplace, their profession, or their pastimes. It's only once they have a well-developed

social network that they're really able to relax and enjoy the relationships that they've so carefully cultivated.

One reason that Twos need to organize their social network is
that they're part of the Heart triad (Types 2-3-4). Heart types tend
to be preoccupied with the question, "Who am I?" Twos answer this
question by seeing who they are in the eyes of other people. And they
can't do this unless they have others around them who are able to mir-
ror back their responses, especially their emotions. Without that mir-
roring, they feel as though they're floating in some sort of "no man's
land," and tend to push for a response (preferably an affirmation).

Lots of relationships means lots of opportunities for affirmation. This is one reason that Twos are willing to put almost unlimited
amounts of energy into building and maintaining their relationships.
At the same time, because relationships matter so much, Twos can
sometimes go overboard, trying too hard or doing too much for others. They can be so eager to create social ties that it's hard for them
to let a relationship develop on its own, without their purposeful
intervention.

Of course, this desire to engineer relationships makes Twos great
social networkers. They know just how to create situations that help
people relax and talk to one another. They know just how to make
people feel at ease, because of their talent for attuning to others'
needs. At the same time, it's this very attunement to others that can
make it hard for them to disengage when they really need to.

Thus, the challenge for Twos is to develop the kind of objectivity
that can provide the counterbalance for their natural subjectivity, so
that the tendency to literally immerse themselves in their relationships is balanced by the discernment necessary to know when to let
go (or when to let the other person take the initiative). John Gray (of
"Mars and Venus" fame) alludes to this challenge of letting go in his
books, noting that there are times when it's best to let a developing
relationship lie fallow, neither pursuing it nor withdrawing from it. In
this way, the relationship either deepens over time or gradually fades
away. If it continues to develop, you know you've got something real,
not false.

This can be a hard lesson for Twos to learn. But when it comes
to devotion, they have few equals. It can be a real strength at Two, a

saving grace. One thinks of the work of Mother Teresa with the dying or the efforts of Princess Diana to ban land mines. Both are considered to be Twos by most enneagram writers. And both were able to find a way to channel their deep desire to reach out to people in a truly unselfish manner. This kind of unselfishness arises not out of some sense of inflation or grandiosity but out of the simple joy of service. Twos have a particular capacity to develop this kind of service ethic because of their naturally tender hearts.

Devotion is a traditionally feminine virtue. Under the right conditions, it develops gradually over time, as an individual matures. When the time is right, it becomes the bud that ripens into a beautiful bloom. It enables wives and mothers (as well as devotional males) to love and nurture others. However, when devotion becomes rigidly enshrined as a societal value for females, the result can be a lot of social pressure for a woman to fulfill the role of devoted helpmate, whether or not she has a devotional nature. When all women are expected to act like Twos (whatever their actual type), the result is seldom a satisfied partner or happy family. Instead, some women never grow up, remaining emotionally dependent throughout their lives; they get what they want by emotional manipulation. Others become angry and resentful, which leads to the kind of passive-aggressive behavior traditionally attributed to mothers-in-law. Even Twos aren't good at playing a devotional role if they're forced to marry too young, because youthful Twos need to find their own identity before cultivating the ability to serve others.

Twos who cultivate self-love and an independent spirit develop the qualities that allow them to genuinely serve others. They become the kind of parents, supporters, or humanitarians that inspire the other eight types to give more freely.

Years ago, I was in a networking group organized by a man who was a Two. He exuded compassion but was at the same time genuinely humble. Everybody loved him. One day, after I'd known him for a long time, he shyly confided to me, "I am a world server."

And he really was. He devoted his whole life to service. He established one of the first neighborhood advocacy groups in the nation. He established a community garden at a time when nobody had ever thought to do this sort of thing (this was in the 1960s). He did countless other things to help people out and to establish innovative models to show people what community is all about. When he got married, he turned the same sort of devoted attention to his family. He never sought any kind of thanks for his work—seeing the fruits of his labor was enough for him.

This man always inspired me. He still does.

My friend's passion was creating large-scale social networks. It brought out all of his talents, all of his creativity. Thinking about him made me realize that, for Twos, making connections between people is a creative act, an act that's intrinsically rewarding—once the Two has acquired the confidence to act independently.

I once saw a Two describe a situation where she had served a group well but experienced social ostracism due to a misunderstanding. This had obviously been a painful experience for her, but she spoke of it with great dignity, without anger or resentment. When I looked at her, I saw someone who had faced her worst nightmare and found the inner resources to stand alone.

Twos who have found themselves and developed the strength to give gladly (but without strings) can make the world a warmer, friendlier place to live.

Type 3: The Self-tester

Threes are pragmatic "doers" whose desire to excel knows no bounds. Like Twos, they tend to be extroverted and outgoing, but their focus is more on tasks and less on people. However, they *do* make an effort to get along with people and adapt to their needs. But their focus is less on the personal dimensions of these relationships and more on their own goals and projects.

Threes tend to be ambitious, hard-working, and able to sacrifice to achieve their goals. They focus more on the material world than unseen realities. For this reason, they can be perceived as insensitive by those who are less materially-oriented and more intuitive.

But Threes usually have great physical stamina and the ability to take a task to completion, no matter how tough. (When I think of Threes, I always envision interns on 36-hour shifts. This makes sense, since it's pretty common for Threes to become physicians.)

The downside of the Three's goal-orientation is a tendency to forget everything but the task, which results in a lot of "Type A" behavior and a difficulty in making time for family and friends. So Threes sometimes need a wake-up call (like physical illness) to make them realize that life is more than a series of tasks and projects. After listening to a panel of Threes, I once asked one of the participants how she knew when to stop working. She got a funny look on her face—it sort of clouded over—and she finally stammered, "I don't."

This eloquently sums up the dilemma of the Three: how to aspire without burning out, how to "go, go, go" (but with exuberance, not compulsion), and how to stop and smell the roses (and actually enjoy the experience). Threes just don't seem to have an "off" button—they go and go until it's impossible to go anymore.

A Three once remarked that the reason she was studying the enneagram was that she'd achieved everything she'd ever wanted by the time she was 30—so what else was there? That's what she wanted to discover. She realized she needed to look beyond the obvious to find out what else life had to offer.

Before I knew the enneagram, I thought that Threes were basically perfect. (Could it be because my mom was a Three?) Whatever the reason, I saw Threes as incredibly competent, put-together, and unflappable—as people that could fit in just about anywhere and do just about anything. My own family conditioning aside, this is the image that Threes project—and it's hard not to see it as real.

Of course, there's nothing actually wrong with projecting an image; we all do this to one extent or another. Even my shy Five friends do it (as best they can) when interviewing for a job or participating in social gatherings. We need a persona to move around in the world, so persona itself is not the problem: our image can be a playful extension of ourselves that we put on like clothing.

What *can* be a problem is getting lost in the persona—getting so identified with it that we lose ourselves in the process. This happens more easily to Threes because they know how to polish their persona in a way that attracts a lot of positive attention. It gets them a lot of good stuff—money, attention, advancement. In short, the Good Life.

What it doesn't get them is Self. When you're 25, this might not matter so much. But when you get to be 35, 45, 55...well, you get the picture. Threes are one of the types (like Sevens) that can really hit a wall at some point in their lives, when they start to realize that life can be perfect and still lack something vital.

Best-selling author Sylvia Brown writes about 30+ life paths possible for a person. One of the most difficult, she says, is the Success path. We all think that successful people have it made. But it's not that easy to be successful. Aside from handling the envy of less successful people—which is not easy—successful people have to eventually sort out the difference between outer success and inner satisfaction. Often, they get a wake-up call in the form of a mid-life crisis precipitated by the realization that life is no longer a joyful experience. This is not an easy juncture for anybody, especially for somebody who has a lot to lose. (Not to mention the fact that the successful person who has an identity crisis doesn't get much sympathy from the rest of us.)

So Point 3 holds interesting and unusual challenges. At enneagram events, Threes bring a uniquely practical perspective that helps ground these events in ordinary reality. Take the example of Richard Groves, a Northwest enneagram teacher who uses the enneagram to support people undergoing big life transitions.

I attended one of his introductory workshops in Seattle. It was a model of what a good workshop should be: informative, well-organized, and sensitively run. It included both a book containing a well-known enneagram test and a beautifully put-together booklet containing his Power Point slides with an area for notes. During his talk, Richard managed to cite just about every well-known teacher in the field. He made sure to include their insights and give credit where credit is due. His efficient, cooperative approach made the event a pleasure to attend. This was a Three at his best.

On Gurdjieff's enneagram, Point 3 is one of the three shock points—places where there are special tests or difficulties to surmount. At Three, the challenge is to ultimately see though the very image that has brought them success, a task that requires the Three to develop the curiosity and spunk to look beyond the need to succeed.

Type 4: The Deep Sea Diver

Fours are sometimes called Romantics or Tragic Romantics. But while Fours tend to be intense and dramatic, they aren't really all that romantic. I call Fours the Deep Sea Diver because this label captures a quality that all Fours seem to share: the compelling desire to look beneath the surface of life.

Fours never accept anything at surface value, but instead delve to see what is really there, deep beneath the waves. Emotionally sensitive, they can be like a psychic sponge, readily picking up the feelings and attitudes of those around them. Fours are also able to detect discrepancies between projected images and authentic feelings. This makes them prone to moodiness or emotional overload, which is often best handled by spending time apart from other people.

Fours are also sensitive to aesthetics. They tend to notice colors, fabrics, textiles, and other aesthetic dimensions of the environment. So they find it unpleasant to spend any amount of time in environments that they deem ugly, plastic, or otherwise unaesthetic. A group of Fours having lunch together at an enneagram event once discovered that they'd all been mentally redecorating the unattractive room in which the event was held.

Fours often feel misplaced when forced to be in situations where the things they value (depth, authenticity, the arts) are not valued by others. Situations like these can make them feel despondent and in need of escape. Motivated by the desire to connect with what is real and authentic in life, they are often willing to sacrifice a great deal to make this connection. They're usually happiest when doing original work that expresses what they feel inside; they are often talented writers, painters, or actors who are not afraid to draw upon their deep emotions for creative purposes.

One thing which I once heard about Fours as creators is that their work is autobiographical—that it always bears the stamp of their individuality. This may be why another common label for Fours is the Individualist. However, while Fours value their individuality, they may look more ruggedly individualistic than other types simply because they feel more compelled to follow the dictates of their inner muse than the dictates of social convention. When they dress in ways that are quirky or unusual, it doesn't necessarily mean they're trying to seek attention. It may be that they find the need to follow their natural aesthetic more compelling than the need to follow current fashion trends.

People get fascinated with the intensity and passion of the Four, being both attracted to it and put off by it. This puts the Four in a double bind, because sometimes she's rewarded for her passion and at other times made to feel that it's over the top. This creates a sort of "push-pull" scenario that's not easy for the Four to handle. At the same time, it's true that Fours can become overly self-dramatizing. When this happens, they may try to draw others into their life dramas (this is probably most true of Sexual Fours—see Chapter 6).

But even the most well-balanced Fours can exhaust types with less intensity, thereby leading those individuals to withdraw. This is probably one reason why Fours can develop feelings of abandonment. They actually do have the kind of energy that can be hard for other types to handle. So they are well-advised to learn ways to curb the effect of their intensity on others; this is a problem they share with Eights (although the intensity of the Eight is more earthy and has less of a "feeling" tone).

Fours are usually aware that others find them too intense. They try to deal with it, but it's not easy, because they have to choose between being themselves (but potentially alienating to others) and curbing their passion (which makes them more socially acceptable but creates a sense of self-alienation). This conflict can be exhausting. It may be one reason that Fours tend to shy away from social events, especially large-scale social functions. They can usually fit in if they really need to, but it's not an appealing way to pass the time.

Fours are probably who Freud had in mind when he posited the existence of a death instinct. Fours are seldom repelled by topics such as death; the main thing that really turns them off is insincerity or superficiality. Melanie Klein, the psychoanalyst who took up where Freud left off, seems to have been a "Four's Four" who saw small babies as consumed by fantasies of sex and death. Anne Rice, another

Four, is also a figure who explores the darker side of human nature, although in a more literary and less morbid fashion than Klein. (This affinity for the depths is usually stronger in Fours who have a Five wing; both Klein and Rice seem likely candidates.)

I once saw a panel of Fours queried as to their occupation. It turned out that four out of five did work requiring them to provide emotional support to people in crisis situations (for example, working in a hospice, manning suicide hot lines, or offering crisis counseling). So while Fours are not much for small talk, they can be extraordinarily attentive when listening to people with serious troubles to share.

Fours and Fives are both what people call "Bottom of the Enneagram" types—and are subject to the effects of the energies in that region of the enneagram. There seems to be some sort of energy vacuum or vortex existing at the bottom of the enneagram (as reflected by the lack of connecting lines there). Both Fours and Fives feel the effects of this region, which seems both chaotic and dynamic. It attunes these types to the kind of primal, creative energy that makes originality possible. But it also makes them sensitive and in need of more rest and time alone than other types.

Because Fours are a Heart type, people expect them to be more emotional than mental. But Fours can be more analytical than people expect, especially if they have a Five wing. Fours can be especially talented at synthesizing ideas and communicating them in writing. They're often better writers than speakers, because writing can be done alone, without the distraction of the audience's emotional reaction to the speaker's presentation. When they interact with people directly, Fours often like to assume the role of teacher, because it gives them the authority to act in response to their inner promptings.

While Fours may not be particularly easy-going or light-hearted, they're seldom dull. Their creativity, originality, and intensity always leave an impression on the people around them. Also, they're one of the few types that are willing and able to deal with intense emotions, psychological traumas, and spiritual crises. What they need to cultivate is the kind of transpersonal outlook that can help them mine the depths without getting trapped in them.

Type 5: The Puzzle-solver

Like Fours, Fives occupy the bottommost place on the enneagram, and also live "in the depths." But where Fours are in a deeply personal emotional space, Fives are in a deeply private mental space. Within that space, they explore how things work, what makes things tick. Not on the surface, but on the most fundamental level imaginable.

Fives tend to be highly analytical. They're encyclopedic in their approach to learning, focusing on both the big picture and the tiny details. They have excellent powers of concentration, so they can get completely wrapped up in whatever topic interests them. Introverted and shy, they don't always know how to take the first step in relating to other people. But they're always pleased when their knowledge is appreciated by others (though they may not show it). Underneath their shyness is a person who's not easily swayed by public opinion and can be rock solid when it comes to standing by core ideas and values.

Fives are often regarded as impractical by other people. But they're only impractical so far as certain things are concerned—like social chit-chat or doing things to impress others. They're not actually trying to flaunt convention; it's just that they have a hard time conjuring up any real concern over such things. They're so focused on their particular area of study that they don't pay a lot of attention to things beyond the scope of their interests.

But when they *do* get interested in something, they're usually quite good at figuring it out, whether it's a calculus equation or something more ordinary. For instance, a Five friend of mine recently came to visit for a few days. During that time, I bought a new portable vacuum. I got it home and plugged it in, but couldn't figure out how to pry it loose from its charger. The usual way—horizontally sliding it forward—didn't work and I was afraid of doing anything too violent lest I break it. I had the cable guy who was connecting my wireless modem look at it, too. He couldn't figure it out, either. I finally called the vacuum cleaner company and they told me what to do—simply lift it straight up and pull hard. When my Five friend came home, I was curious to see how quickly he could solve the problem. Within a half a minute, he'd discovered the solution. How did he do it? I don't know. But he's always had a knack for problem solving.

That's why I call Type 5 the Puzzle-solver. Fives have this amazing ability to deconstruct reality and put it back together in a whole new way. They're often called Observers, which is also an accurate descriptor. But it doesn't say what they are actually doing when they watch. We might think they're simply having an attack of shyness. But they're not just being shy—they're actively absorbing information which they may later put to use in some ingenious and unconventional way.

What's hard for Fives is to share the information they collect with other people—at least, to share it in a way that other people understand. Fives tend to be complex reasoners, but they often find it difficult to convert their intricate understanding into a form that makes it intelligible to the rest of us. One problem is that this translation process can "dumb down" the information so much that it loses much of its worth, at least from the Five's point of view. So Fives have little incentive to attempt such a translation. But when they do have the incentive, they can be very effective teachers. They just have to take the same ability that enables them to understand new ideas and apply it to develop good communication skills.

Most Fives love games, any kind of games—card games, computer games, video games, or chess. They're pretty cutthroat players, too, demonstrating that beneath that quiet exterior lurks a surprisingly competitive spirit, although one more geared to competing for intellectual bragging rights than acquiring worldly goods. It's not that Fives are averse to riches, it's just that they're more intrigued by knowledge than goods.

Fives are known for their lack of emotionality, but they're not so much lacking in emotion as lacking in the ability to project their feelings to others. Also, they tend to be compartmentalized. This means that their emotions are there but may be hard to immediately access (especially for Fives with a Six wing). I once sat in on a fascinating discussion between a Two therapist and several Fives on a type panel. The Two found the Fives' seeming lack of emotional response unnerving and didn't know how to deal with it. How could she work with somebody like this in therapy?

The Fives had some ideas about this. They said that it was important to understand that the lack of emotional expressiveness doesn't reflect a lack of feeling. It's more like the feelings of Fives are so deep and unwavering that they change slowly, like the seasons—not quickly, like the weather. The Fives on the panel expressed puzzlement about how most people could change their feelings so fast. To work with a Five in therapy, they said, the therapist would have to let go of the need to elicit an immediate emotional response. She would have to allow the Five to access his emotions in a way that makes sense to *him*—and to give up the need to establish an immediate emotional connection.

Fives always have interesting things to say, and they say them in unconventional (and sometimes obscure) ways. They often have a childlike quality, although they can be stubborn, too. If a Five decides he doesn't want to do something, nothing in this world or the next will force him to do it. Of course, he won't tell you this. He'll simply fail to respond—perhaps indefinitely.

Fives seem to be in touch with something deep inside that sustains and refreshes them. This is one reason they are often seen as shamanic. Even Fives that aren't into the idea of shamanism still have this ability to go to the roots of a problem. It's what gives them the ability to "think outside the box." Their challenge is to find some way of connecting with others, so they can participate in the community that lies beyond their mental world.

Type 6: The Steward

Like Fours and Fives, Sixes are aware of the deeper currents in life. But they're typically less comfortable with these currents and more apt to try to tune them out. Perhaps this is because they too easily tune into the potential for untoward happenings and hidden dangers. Sixes are often preternaturally sensitive and can be quite psychic. But they also get their signals crossed at times, and this tends to keep them off-balance and makes it hard for them to have complete confidence in their intuitions.

Sixes may cover up this lack of confidence with a skeptical or even cynical demeanor. Although this skepticism can make them hold back at times, it can also help them notice what's likely to go wrong in a situation and work hard to prevent this from happening. But this is not always what they do. Sometimes they react to fear by "going where angels fear to tread," heading straight for whatever they fear the most, in an effort to conquer fear itself. This can bounce them into just the kind of situation they most want to avoid.

Sixes value loyalty and tradition; they often assume the role of "defenders of the faith" and champions of the underdog. They're the most service-oriented of the types and sometimes take on thankless jobs that nobody else wants to touch, which is why I call Type Six the Steward.

Sixes are perhaps the hardest people for others to type (although Nines can also be tough to type).* When Sixes are introduced to a new system like the enneagram, they don't usually jump on board right away. They hold back, waiting to see whether this new thing is really all it's cracked up to be. Only when they're sure it's not a scam do they get curious and begin to open up.

When we try to pin down a Six (or even when Sixes try to do this for themselves), it can be a tricky business, especially if we try to do it by looking at behavior instead of energy. This is because the behavior of Sixes can be all over the board; the behavior we see depends on how they choose to deal with agitation—by becoming overly placating, getting combative, or holding tightly onto social conventions. These behaviors all represent efforts to come to terms with their natural sense of trepidation.

But the Six *must* come to terms with this energy, because Point 6 is the second shock point on the enneagram. At the enneagram shock points, it's necessary to come to terms with some problem or

---

*Sixes are hard to type because they don't want to identify with *any* type; Nines are hard to type because they want to identify with *every* type!

tendency before we can move on to a new phase in our lives. For the Six, this means letting go of fear and doubt (or at least being willing to act in spite of them). It's for good reason that Point 6 has been called the place where we meet the Dweller on the Threshold.

Non-Sixes tend to think of Sixes as having an overactive imagination. They seldom consider the possibility that Sixes are actually tuning into some hidden dimension of life that has valuable lessons to teach us—if only we had the same sensitivity as the Six. It's my sense that Sixes are not inherently more fearful than other types. It's just that they are more in touch with the kind of energies that would promote fear in any rational person.

The fact that the rest of us fail to "tune in" is also alarming from the Six's point of view—it reminds me of a movie I saw where the protagonist was picking up bad vibes from the environment without really understanding why. He thought he must be crazy until he got hold of some special glasses that enabled him to see mind-numbing messages (like "Conform!", "Follow orders!", or "Obey!") being subliminally projected to everybody in his city. He wasn't crazy after all—people really *were* out to get him!

Although most people think of fear as something to be rid of, there are actually positive aspects of fear that are under-appreciated. For example, fear is a close cousin to awe. And cultivating a sense of awe can help us appreciate life in a deeper, more profound fashion. Fear also gives us an incentive to get along with others, especially to form cooperative social networks. And it helps us develop respect and combat cynicism, because we can't really be fearful and cynical at the same time.

The difficulty for Types 4, 5, and 6 is that they are all tuning into something that is in some way "from the depths." As a result, these types don't always have an easy time relating to people whose energy is less subterranean. If we think of the enneagram as a progression from 1-2-3 to 4-5-6 to 7-8-9, the 4-5-6 sequence happens in the middle of the process—and this is the place in a process, a story, or a play when there is always some sort of mid-life crisis, descent into the underworld, or other seemingly insurmountable difficulty. What is more, Point 6 is the *last* step in this process—the place where we have to make a final and irrevocable commitment to whatever task we have taken on. So is it really so strange that the Six feels afraid?

Although fear is not an easy energy to work with, the Six who is willing to consciously face her fears becomes a pioneer who can show the rest of us how to transform fear into faith and doubt into understanding. She can learn how to courageously move ahead, despite her fears—and how to do it by navigating a course between two extremes (crazy courage and rigid conformity). When she's able to do this— to become aware of fear, accept it, and allow it to "settle in"—fear gradually loses its power to terrorize.

Overcoming fear can be tremendously empowering for the Six. Not only does she cease seeing fear as the enemy—but she gains the ability to help other people come to terms with *their* fears. In this way, she takes on the role of a true steward of life, creating faith and hope wherever she goes.

Type 7: The Improviser

Sevens are the most exuberant of all the types, having an unexcelled ability to make work into play and to notice the brighter side of any situation. They're usually more extroverted than introverted, and tend to have an extended community of acquaintances. Sevens also tend to be unconventional, so they like to develop new or unusual ways of relating to other people. During the 1960s, they were the original flower children and slightly later, the New Age visionaries.

Like Threes, Sevens are always in motion. But unlike Threes, Sevens need to make their work fun. Otherwise, they find it hard to bring tasks to completion. Once they get bored, they tend to get distracted. While they can obviously benefit from getting more focused and disciplined, they usually have a hard time drumming up much interest in that sort of thing. They need some sort of attractive incentive to remain focused.

I call Sevens the Improviser because they are really good at "winging it"—at taking on tasks they don't know how to do but finding a way to do them anyway, somehow pulling the know-how virtually out of the air. Their talent for improvising is a natural extension of their ability to be a "quick study."

A Seven friend of mine was once asked whether she knew how to cook professionally in a restaurant. She said yes, even though she didn't. But amazingly enough, she and another friend somehow managed to do all the cooking for a few months without running the restaurant into the ground. She said it was fun!

Sevens really do seem to have more fun than other types. And they seem to know ways to transform ordinary tasks into something enjoyable. The film *Life is Beautiful* really captures the joie de vivre we see at Point 7—it's the story of the misadventures of a zany Italian Jew in the 1940s (who is a pretty obvious Seven). Unfortunately, the film takes a tragic turn when he and his young son wind up in a concentration camp. But the father is determined to protect his child, so he tells him that the concentration camp is just a big game, where children can gain points to win a military tank. It's a sweet and touching tale, and it really captures the way that Sevens can potentially transform the sorrows of life into events that touch the heart.

More than other types, Sevens tend to change over time. When they're young, they have the kind of high-flying energy and exuberance that knows no bounds. The combination of high energy and low focus pushes them out into life, where they try to taste everything that it has to offer—and to do it all at once! The phrase "burning the candle at both ends" was probably coined with Sevens in mind.

As they grow older, many Sevens find it easier to get grounded and focused, although the interest in multi-tasking (or more properly, "multi-playing") usually remains. I once watched a type panel with two Sevens, one in her mid-forties and the other about 20 years old. The older Seven knew a lot about the enneagram while the younger knew very little. The older one said that she basically thought she could do anything in her life until she hit 40; her life seemed charmed. At that point, she tried to get pregnant. And she couldn't. She tried and tried, and it didn't happen. This came as a great shock to her—for the first time in her life, she hit an obstacle that she couldn't float over, duck under, or avoid. She said it was a real wake-up call. Meanwhile, the other panelist—the 20-year-old—was looking more and more bewildered. He'd come to sit on the panel as a favor to one of the workshop leaders, and he didn't know much about Sevens. He was obviously confused to hear that his sunny disposition and soaring energy could be any sort of problem.

At another enneagram event, I heard a Seven in his 70s observe that he was just beginning to learn how to settle down and work on just one project at a time. It still wasn't easy but he had enough insight to take on the challenge.

Sevens are probably the most popular type on the enneagram. Generally speaking, they're the kind of people we like to have around—funny, entertaining, charming, and flexible. They're interested in just about everything and everybody, so when we're in the company of a Seven, it can be like standing in bright sunshine.

Sevens are often blessed with many talents. And they seem lucky in a way that's the envy of their friends. But just as with Threes, too much success is not always a good thing. Neither is too much talent. I've met more than one Seven who finds it difficult to stick with a job that they don't like—it's just too easy to find another. I once talked to a Seven (a very personable, attractive gentleman) who'd managed to procure 15 or 20 responsible managerial positions *in the past three years.* It was hard to believe he'd actually done it—can you imagine what he said about his job history during his interviews? But somehow, he'd pulled it off. When I asked him why he kept leaving all these jobs, fear came into his eyes and he looked down. He finally said, "Well, it's like riding a roller-coaster. It's great going up the incline, but once I get to the top, I like to jump off before it goes down again."

Another Seven friend has so many talents that she doesn't know what to do with them. She's so good at so many things that she can't settle down and pick one on which to concentrate. She gets caught up in one activity and then another. She gets restless and can't settle down. At the same time, she's impulsive and feels unhappy if she can't have whatever she wants right away (probably due to an Eight wing), so she runs up debts buying clothing or paying for massage treatments or other body work. The idea of "doing without" doesn't occur to her. Or if it does, it's quickly rejected. After overspending, she feels guilty but still unable to muster the resolve needed to stop spending.

Some Sevens do manage to find constructive ways to channel their restless energy. Another friend of mine is a psychotherapist, group leader, and fitness instructor. She's able to set her own schedule and does enough different activities to satisfy the Seven's need for diversity and novelty. At the same time, she's grounded enough to reign herself in when her desire for novelty outstrips her time, energy, and financial resources. But she sometimes feels exhausted by the need to live up to the Seven's reputation for high-powered enthusiasm. "Sure I'm 'up' a lot of the time, but not all the time. There are times when I feel depressed or tired, just like anybody else. But if I act that way, people don't like it—they like the 'happy me', not the 'sad me'."

It can be hard to allow our Seven friends to really be themselves. But it's important that we do, because otherwise we make it hard for them to stop dancing 24 hours a day. Because Sevens are highly impressionable, it's important for their friends to support their need to wind down (instead of forcing them to play the role of entertainer all the time).

Of course, the Seven eventually has to learn to take responsibility for himself, even in the absence of input from others. This is a big step for someone whose energy is so "up in the air." He may not be able to take this step until late in life, when he's finally collected enough experiences that he's able to focus more on *appreciating* and less on *accumulating*.

Type 8: The Master

Eights are like a force of nature—big, strong, and totally grounded in physical reality. Even when they're not physically big, their aura of command makes them seem larger than life. They're natural leaders but can have difficulty taking a subordinate role unless the boss is somebody they really respect. They can also find it difficult to truly appreciate the efforts of others, especially people who lack their vigor and independence.

Eights can also find it hard to let down their guard enough to have a truly intimate relationship, in large part because their tough exterior hides an incredibly tender heart—so tender in fact that they seldom dare show it. Also, because they tend to be blunt, Eights can trigger a defensive reaction from other people. And this reaction can increase their own defensiveness and the sense that people are more hostile than friendly. So they need friends and partners who know how to hold their own without overreacting to the Eight's bluster.

Naturally chivalrous, Eights hold values such as honor, courage, and personal loyalty in high esteem; they're the natural protectors of the weak and helpless. If they perceive an injustice, they're quick to react—sometimes too quick. Eights anger easily, and they usually find this anger hard to control. The problem seems to be one of timing. They don't intend to get angry, but it can happen so fast that they tend to blow up first and think later. It's not easy to control their fiery temper. But as Eights age, it becomes easier, both because they gain life skills and because they come to understand the damage that un-controlled anger can inflict.

Eights are usually more at home in the natural world than in the world of ideas or emotions. Like Ones and Nines, they have great gut instincts, and can "suss out" another person pretty rapidly. However, it can be hard for them to express their gut feelings in words. (They clearly know what they know, but don't know *how* they know it.) But that doesn't make them waver. They're in touch with something real and substantial, and the fact that they can't explain it doesn't make them apologize one bit.

Psychic medium John Edward is a gut type—probably a Nine with an Eight wing or vice-versa. On the opening credits of his TV show, he says, "Outside the physical world lies the Other Side, where those who have crossed over [died] continue to live. How do I know? Because I do."

And that's that.

Another example is Cesar Millan, the National Geographic Channel's *Dog Whisperer*. In an article for the *Enneagram Monthly*, I cited him as an example of a well-balanced Eight. Here's how his TV show begins:

[Announcer:] "When good dogs go bad, there's one man who's their best friend." [Cesar's voice cuts in]: "No dog is too much for me. I rehabilitate dogs, I train people. I am the Dog Whisperer."

This might sound like bragging, but it's just the way that Eights talk. They don't mince words. When you see Cesar in action, it's no brag—like most Eights, he delivers the goods. He has the ability to instinctively sense an animal's state and give it the structure and guidance it needs to become "happy, healthy, and well-balanced." I saw him live on stage in Seattle, and he's just as self-possessed and masterful in person as he is on his show.

His disciplined approach is typical of a healthy Eight—there's no messing around; he simply gets the job done. Eights have the kind of determination and sheer force of will necessary to do just about anything they set their minds to. The challenge for them is never a lack of energy or focus—it's a potential lack of control. Like Sevens, they have a lot of energy to manage. Unlike Sevens, they find it easy to focus on one thing at a time and to take a task to completion. But the energy at Point 7 is light and airy; the energy at Point 8 is pure fire—and it's all too easy for the flames to get out of control.

Most Eights need some way to channel their explosive energy so it doesn't build up and cause them problems; usually this means physical activity (martial arts, weight lifting, or other demanding sports). The best combination is some activity which is physically demanding but which also requires mental discipline.

Like Twos (a type to which they are connected), Eights have a certain devotional quality that needs a suitable object of expression. They need a goal, and it has to be a worthy goal—one that inspires them. This can be hard to find in a world where the values so treasured by Eights (like personal honor and courage) now earn so little respect. Threes also like a big goal, but for Threes, high achievement is a means of discovering who they are; for Eights, it's what gives them the incentive to develop leadership skills.

Eights are natural leaders but need to learn how to lead from their heart and head, not just from their gut. When they do this, they achieve the kind of mastery required to handle their "big" energy.

That's why I call Eight the Master. Point 8 is clearly the place of mastery—the place that represents (or ought to represent) the culmination of the lessons learned at all the other eight positions on the enneagram. At Point 8, mastery is clearly a "must do" situation, because with so much energy concentrated in one place, you either have mastery or tyranny, whether at the level of the family, the community, or the nation.

But tyranny does not fulfill the tyrant—it only gives him a way to vent his rage. When he has nothing left to destroy, he destroys himself. And this is why it's important not to allow the Eights we love to dominate us. We can help them (and ourselves) by mustering up the fortitude necessary to support them without allowing them to call all the shots.

Type 9: The Storyteller

Nines have a way of bringing people together. Although they can seem almost invisible in a group, at the same time they quietly radiate an aura of palpable peace and calm that brings people into harmony. Although they're often called mediators, most Nines actually don't much like to mediate—they'd rather avoid conflict situations altogether. It's the *other* eight types that appreciate the Nine's ability and encourage him to assume this peacemaking role.

I call Type 9 the Storyteller because it's often through storytelling that Nines find it possible to express who they are. Point 9 on the enneagram is a place of creative possibility, which is probably why Nines usually like stories better than factual accounts. Facts describe the world as it is; stories describe the world of our imagination.

The stories that Nines tell don't seem to be so much deliberately composed as channeled from some invisible part of themselves. These stories are often fantasies or fairy tales and are archetypal in nature. The down side of this preoccupation with fantasy is the Nineish tendency to get lost in fantasy and simply imagine how they would like things to be as opposed to making them happen in reality. Nines can also get caught up in TV watching (or some other activity that allows them to zone out) and lose many hours without quite realizing where the time went.

Nines are by nature receptive to other people's ideas. But they can find it more difficult to appreciate their own (although this is less true of Nines with an Eight wing). It's for this reason that Nines are often difficult to type. They identify with the characteristics of all the nine types. But they can have a hard time noticing what distinguishes them from other individuals.

Nines often find it hard to take sides because they don't have a really strong sense of which side is best; *all* the sides have some kind of valid point. This is one reason why decision-making can be the bane of their existence. They often rely on friends to help them come to a decision because they find it so difficult to do this on their own. This is especially true when it comes to personal decisions, because it can be hard for a Nine to know what he really wants for himself. Friends who know him well can help him by supporting his decision-making process, but without making the decisions for him.

Another reason that decision making is difficult is that decisions bring change, and Nines don't like change much. Also, decision making makes them aware of their separateness from other people. So when a choice is required, the Nine typically hangs back, procrastinating for as long as possible

As a result, Nines seldom arrive promptly on time for events. They tend to be late (although some Nines arrive early, in order to compensate for their tendency toward lateness). Although Nines can be on time when it really matters (for example, when they're catching a plane), it's never easy for them. During work, they may be able to rise to the occasion. But after work, they tend to slip into a zone of "no time" and handle their social engagements accordingly.

Even at work, being on time isn't easy. One of my Nine friends gradually converted her 9-to-5 job to a noon-to-nine job, but often ended up staying until 10, 11, or even midnight. It was hard to get going, but even harder to stop. Another friend has an early morning job and routinely arrives 5 or 10 minutes late.

Nines can be quite bright, but most often, they do not *live* in their intellect but in a simpler, more elemental part of the self—a part that is closer to the natural world. Nines enjoy simple things and simple living. On the other hand, they tend to accumulate clutter. While not all Nines have problems with too much stuff, many do. It's a tendency that they share with Fives. But while Fives accumulate stuff in order to build a knowledge base (and maybe to create an insulating wall), Nines accumulate stuff because they just don't get around to sorting through things.

Nines usually present a calm exterior to the world, although they report that the appearance of outer calmness does not mean they feel peaceful inside. They are, after all, a gut type, and these types all have a temper. Every so often, it can make a sudden (and often explosive) appearance. I once saw a normally placid Nine suddenly blow up at an Eight who had been persistently pushing on him. The moral? You can only push a Nine so far before he pushes back. And when he does, he often pushes back quite forcefully!

While it can be hard for Nines to get themselves in gear, once they get moving, they're hard workers. It's just difficult for them to stay on track, so completing tasks can often take awhile. To keep from getting off track, they seek to develop routines and habits that can keep them moving through their day. But they have to be careful to take breaks; like Threes, they can get into the habit of working without stopping, not realizing where the time went.

Both Sevens and Nines have a childlike quality (Sevens are often called the Peter Pans of the enneagram). But while Sevens are child-like in their ability to transform work into play, Nines are childlike in their openness and sense of wonder. It's this openness that allows Nines to take the perspective of other people. The challenge for them is to retain their childlike qualities without sacrificing the ability to deal with situations that require a more mature response.

Nines make good friends, because they really appreciate anything you do for them. They have generous hearts and give freely of their time and energy. The problem is that they often forget their personal needs in the process. They need to be encouraged to do things just for themselves, not somebody else. And they also need to be allowed to get cranky and out of sorts (rather than having to be "nice" all the time), so they get in touch with the objectionable emotions that they find all too easy to push away.

− 3 −

Energy Centers

The enneagram has three main energy centers: the Heart Center, the Head Center, and the Body/Gut Center. These correspond to energy centers discussed by G. I. Gurdjieff, who was the first to publicly disseminate the teachings on the enneagram. The energy centers were later mapped onto the enneagram as follows:

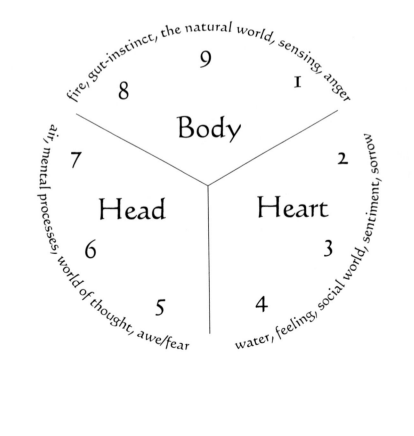

Since each of us has a mind, emotions, and a body, we obviously have all three energy centers within us. At the same time, one of these centers is most dominant for each of us. It's the center in which our point of view (type) is located:

- Types 8 – 9 – 1 are in the *Body Center*
- Types 2 – 3 – 4 are in the *Heart Center*
- Types 5 – 6 – 7 are in the *Head Center*

Different enneagram teachers discuss the centers in different ways. Most enneagram teachers at least give a nod to the centers, because they offer such a useful framework for understanding the nine types. The main qualities of each center are shown below.

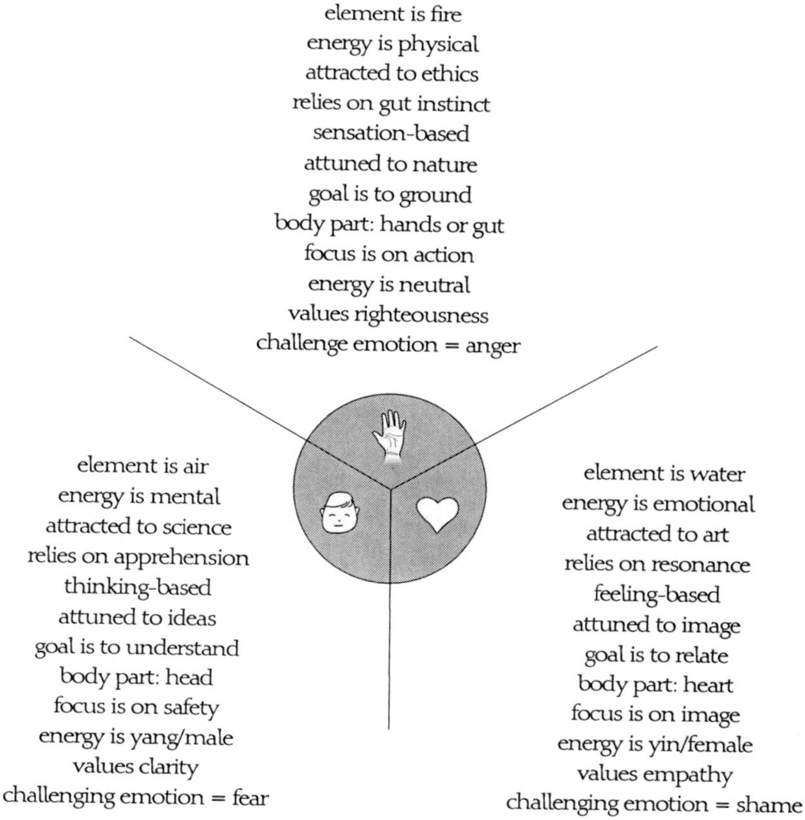

element is fire
energy is physical
attracted to ethics
relies on gut instinct
sensation-based
attuned to nature
goal is to ground
body part: hands or gut
focus is on action
energy is neutral
values righteousness
challenge emotion = anger

element is air
energy is mental
attracted to science
relies on apprehension
thinking-based
attuned to ideas
goal is to understand
body part: head
focus is on safety
energy is yang/male
values clarity
challenging emotion = fear

element is water
energy is emotional
attracted to art
relies on resonance
feeling-based
attuned to image
goal is to relate
body part: heart
focus is on image
energy is yin/female
values empathy
challenging emotion = shame

I always think in terms of the energy centers when initially trying to help somebody determine their type. Why? Because it's easier to focus on three energy types than nine enneagram types. We can start by looking at someone's energy, to see whether it is mainly

- gutty, practical, and no-nonsense (Body Center)
- hearty, emotive, and interactive (Heart Center)
- detached, intellectual, and "up in the air" (Head Center)

This approach works particularly well for identifying the hexad types (Types 1-4-2-8-5-7), because they exhibit the energy of the center in a pretty obvious way. It also works for the inner triangle types (Types 3-6-9), but in a more subtle way, for reasons we'll talk about later in this chapter.

Body Center

The energy of the Body Center is fiery and creative in nature, like lava. It's hot and volatile also but part of the earth. It flows when it's hot but solidifies when it cools off.

Because this energy emanates from the gut, it serves as our main source of bodily vitality. It's what gives us the ability to be aware of our bodies in a tangible, visceral way, so we can ground ourselves in physical reality. It also enables us to tap into the instinctive side of life, especially the natural world.

Using a slightly different analogy, the energy from this center is *nuclear* in nature—it's the power that comes from the nucleus of our being, especially our physical being. It's instinctual and survival-oriented, and it keeps us alert to what's happening in the here and now, so we can preserve the physical vehicle that makes life possible.

Body/gut energy gives us the ability to feel alert to what's happening in the physical environment. When there's too little, we feel a lack of vitality and a sense of disconnection from our body and the physical world. When there's too much, we feel over-amped and restless. The energy becomes hard to control, because it's expansive, intense, and naturally explosive. It can erupt like lava out of a volcano, spewing forth into the air: what it touches, it burns.

Body Center types (8-9-1) have this fire energy in abundance. It gives them a special potential to attune to their gut instinct and to draw sustenance directly from the natural world. At the same time, it makes it hard for them to have a real sense of interiority—that is, to experience their inner selves as tangible and real. Why? Because there's so much fire inside them that it's hard to make out the shape of the inner self.

In order to experience this inner self, they need to find some way to bank the inner fire, so it doesn't consume them. Only then does it become a warming, vital energy that can sustain them without obscuring their subtler qualities or sense of selfhood.

Heart Center

The energy of the Heart Center is like water—free-flowing, downward-moving, and refreshing. It's shaped by whatever contains it, which is why Heart Types seek interaction with others: it's how they gain a sense of who they are and where they belong.

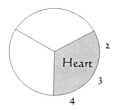

Like water, Heart Center energy seeps into the earth, creating the conditions that bring about new life. So it has a nourishing, generative quality that supports creation. In this sense, it is feminine in nature. The energy of the Heart Center is what gives us *heart*—that quality of being that enables us to stay in touch with our feelings and to empathize with those we love.

Heart energy enables us to nurture, support, and connect with other people. When there's too little, we become dry, detached, even callous—we lack the ability to feel personally invested in life. When there's too much, we become inundated with it; this makes us feel heavy and weighed-down. If it comes to us suddenly, it can have the power to sweep us off our foundations, like a flood.

Heart Center types (2-3-4) tend to be particularly attuned to the effect of their actions on other people and to the emotional response that their actions elicit. This attunement can make them supportive friends and responsive listeners but also oversensitive to negative feedback, because it's often more unsettling to them than to other types.

Once Heart types get off-track emotionally, it can be hard for them to get on track again. So they may be tempted to find some way to shut off (or at least restrict) the flow of emotions. But shutting down the flow of emotions shuts down the heart; what remains is a false heartiness that's a poor substitute for real feeling. So the challenge for Heart types is to learn how to make friends with strong emotions, so they can let emotional currents flow through them in a way that heals and rejuvenates.

Head Center

The energy of the Head Center is like air: light, cool, and invisible. So it has a subtle quality that can be hard to pin down. It naturally floats above the earth, moving this way and that. At the same time, it can be sharp, like a knife (think of how a cold wind can cut through even the thickest garment). And this airy energy can easily become turbulent when infused with disturbed or sudden feeling.

Mental energy is essentially masculine in nature, and it's what we use to cut through emotional turmoil and gut-level inertia. It helps us separate out the essential from the inessential. It dries us out, lifts us up, and makes us feel lighter and clearer. However, its sharpness requires tempering, so that it doesn't cut people, unintentionally hurting their feelings. It also requires stabilizing (so that a slight sense of agitation doesn't easily get whipped up into a gale-force hurricane of fear and doubt).

Head energy brings clarity and discernment. Too little can make a person foggy, undiscerning, and "heavy" (without lightness or detachment); too much creates aridity, over-detachment, and coldness. It can also make people prone to indulge in mental flights of fancy.

Head Center types (5-6-7) are particularly attuned to mental energy. This gives them the ability to work in the realm of thought and to see ideas from many angles, especially unusual or unconventional angles. At the same time, this mental energy can disconnect them from other people and the natural world unless they make a conscious effort to stay in touch with their feelings and with everyday reality. The goal for Head types is to still the mind and cultivate a sense of detached calmness, so that they gain the clarity needed to use their mental skills in constructive ways.

Fire-Water-Air vs. Anger-Shame-Fear

Up to this point, I've talked about the three centers by referring to the elements of fire, water, and air where *fire* is paired with the Body Center, *water* with the Heart Center, and *air* with the Head Center. The missing element is earth. But is it really missing?

No, it's not. It's represented by the enneagram itself, which serves to ground, contain, and integrate the energies of the individual energy centers. Just as the planet Earth provides a container for human life, the enneagram provides a container for the energies of the three energy centers, each of which has a unique relationship with the earth element. Fire exists in the earth as lava that comes from the core up to

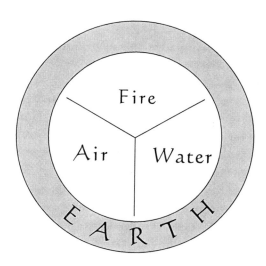

The Enneagram and the Four Elements

the surface; water flows from higher places through channels to the sea; and air circulates freely above and around the earth.

Thus, fire types (8-9-1) are the most "earthed" (grounded); their energy has a natural affinity with the earth, since it arises from deep within it and creates the very crust of which it is composed. Air types (5-6-7) tend to be the least grounded, because air is an element that does not really mix with earth; it just glides over it. Water types (2-3-4) are somewhere in between, because water is distinct from earth but mixes with it quite readily.

Assigning elements to each enneagram triad gives me a means to talk about the energy centers in a value-neutral way. But many discussions on the energy centers are not value-neutral. They focus mostly on three negative emotions—anger, shame, and fear. Here's how this model works:

- body types = *anger* types
- heart types = *shame* types
- head types = *fear* types

When I first studied the enneagram, I was taught about the centers mainly by reference to this anger-shame-fear model. Although this approach can be useful (especially in therapeutic situations), it encourages us to think of the types mainly in terms of their negative emotions, rather than their energetic nature. So it creates a pretty strong negative bias.

While it's true that fire and anger are related, talking about *fire* energy is not quite the same thing as talking about *angry* energy; talking about air and water energy is clearly not the same thing as talking about the emotions of fear and shame, respectively. Fire can become anger—but it can also give us *physical vitality*. Water can become shame—but it can also give us *empathy*. Air can become fear or doubt—but it can also give us *discernment*.

There are many ways to talk about the energy of the centers (see the chart opposite). If the goal is to use that energy for constructive purposes, it's useful to look at it from as many perspectives as possible.

Comparing the Three Energy Centers

DIMENSION ▼	BODY/GUT	HEART	HEAD
ELEMENTAL ENERGY	fire	water	air
ENERGETIC PROPERTY	grounding	circulating	drying
MAIN FOCUS	sensing	feeling	thinking
REFERENCE POINT	nature	people	ideas
POLARITY	neutral	yin/feminine	yang/masculine
MODE OF EXPRESSION	moving	communicating	apprehending
EVOLUTIONARY ROLE	originating	involving	evolving
SOURCE OF INSPIRATION	honor	beauty	intellect
CHALLENGING EMOTION	anger	sorrow/shame	fear/doubt
STRENGTH	righteousness	empathy	brilliance
ACADEMIC FOCUS	ethics	arts	sciences
PLANE OF EXISTENCE	physical	emotional	mental
RESPONSIBILITY	acting	relating	understanding
PATH TO INNER SELF	self-discipline	self-exploration	self-affirmation
RESULTS OF INNER WORK	self-control	self-discovery	self-confidence
SPIRITUAL QUALITY	presence	devotion	contemplation
SOUL DESIRE	oneness	ecstasy	awe

Effect of Position Within the Center

Now that we've looked at how the centers can be described en-
ergetically, let's take a look at the role that each type plays within its
respective center.

Although we have three points of view within each center, each
expresses the energy of that center in a unique way. As I mentioned
a few pages ago, the hexad types (1-4-2-8-5-7) express the energy of
their center in a way that is fairly prototypical while the inner triangle
types (3-6-9) express that energy in a way that can seem atypical or
even the opposite from what we would expect for that center.

This means that, of the three Body types (8-9-1), Types 8 and 1
are most apt to openly exhibit the fiery energy we associate with the
Body center, while Type 9 tends to seem more peaceful and calm. Of
the three Heart types (2-3-4), Types 2 and 4 are more apt to display
emotionality than Type 3. Of the three Head types (5-6-7), Types 5
and 7 are apt to have an obviously heady detachment while Type 6 can
seem more edgy or reactive. Why this discrepancy?

The explanation usually put forth for this discrepancy is psychoanalytic in orientation. Each position within the center is characterized as a form of psychological imbalance which is the result of early
childhood trauma; the nature of the trauma is said to determine the

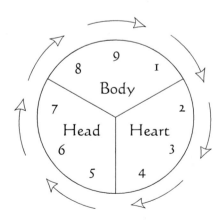

The Flow of Energy Around the Enneagram

kind of energy imbalance. Types at the center midpoints (3-6-9) are said to be psychologically repressed. Types 2-5-8 are said to *over-express* the energy of the center and Types 1-4-7 are said to *under-express* it.

I don't subscribe to this psychoanalytic view. So I needed another way to account for the differences in how each type expresses the energy of its center. The explanation that makes most sense to me is grounded in the process-oriented view of the enneagram that is introduced in Chapter 1 and discussed more fully in Chapter 8.

Briefly, this process-oriented view requires us to see the nine types not only as personality types but as points in a dynamic process, a process that proceeds clockwise around the enneagram: Type 1 represents the beginning of the process, Type 2 represents the second stage, etc., all the way around the enneagram. We can view each energy center as one of three zones that we pass through as we proceed around the circle. Traversing each zone (that is, each center), we're always in one of three positions: (a) moving *into* the center, (b) moving *through* the middle of the center; or (c) moving *out* of a center, as shown on the enneagram below.

On the next page is a discussion of how the position of each type within its center affects the way it expresses that center's energy.

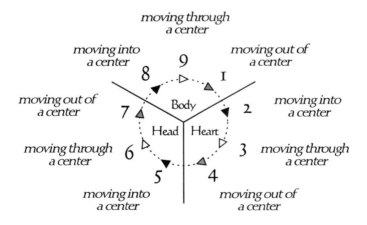

Three Positions within Each Center

Moving INTO a new center = EXPRESSING (Types 2-5-8). These types express the energy of the center in a very obvious and even stereotypical way. That's why they're said to over-express it. But we can see this over-expression as the natural result of arriving in new territory where the energy dynamic is unfamiliar. It's natural for newcomers to initially behave in a way that looks like over-adaptation, because they're trying to immerse themselves in the energy in order to make a successful transition from the old to the new. So what looks like imbalance is simply the conscious effort to adapt to a new situation.

Passing THROUGH the center point = RECEIVING (Types 3-6-9). As we become more familiar with the center's energy, we become adept at expressing that energy in a way that's more refined and less obvious. We become familiar with its subtler (and even hidden) dimensions. By the time we've arrived at the heart of the center, we're like the fish who swims in water without quite realizing the nature of the medium in which it's immersed. We're no longer conscious of the energy as something separate from ourselves; we can thus embody its innermost qualities, which tend to be somewhat different (and less recognizable) than its outer qualities.

Moving OUT OF the center = SYNTHESIZING (Types 1-4-7). As we move into the third position in the center, it's time to pull together the threads of all we've learned. Our task is to integrate (synthesize) the center's inner and outer aspects, combining them in a creative way. At this point, we're also feeling the pull of the next center, so we have to deal with that energy, as well. These competing demands tend to create complexity, restlessness, and an anticipatory spirit.

To summarize this approach: The position of each type within the center determines the way that this type tends to express the energy of the center. Types just entering the center (2-5-8) express the energy in a way that's prototypical for that center and thus hard to miss. Types in the middle of the center (3-6-9) express the energy more subtly or inwardly. Types moving out of the center (1-4-7) express the energy in a way that represents a synthesis between inward and outward expression.

This introduction puts us in a position to see how these two factors—position and center energy—interact to produce the unique energy associated with each type.

Body Types (concrete, grounded, action-oriented)

Type 8 (expressive). As the type that comes first in the Body Center, Eights display the fiery energy of the center in a way that is anything but subtle. Thus, Eights tend to be intense, charismatic, and full of fiery desire that seeks tangible expression in the physical world.

Type 9 (receptive). With an impassive and seemingly imperturbable energy, Nines initially appear to be everything that Eights are not. But despite their outer calm, they're just as much of a gut type as Eights. But because they're at the center's midpoint, their energy is more receptive. So the fire is tamped down, like a glowing ember—but an ember that can definitely flare up, given sufficient provocation.

Type 1 (synthesizing). In Ones, the expressive fire energy of the Eight and the receptive energy of the Nine are synthesized into a form that's highly refined yet taut with tension. Although this isn't an easy energy to work with, it's an energy that can soar to the heights with the sufficient focus and discipline.

Heart Types (circulating, relational, image-oriented)

Type 2 (expressive). As a type just entering the Heart Center, Twos express heart energy in a very obvious, hard-to-miss way. They're very aware of their own feelings and use them to actively reach out to other people, establishing social networks in which they can circulate freely. They best fit our image of what a Heart type would look like.

Type 3 (receptive). With an innate sense of how to navigate a social network, Threes readily adapt to the needs of others, work cooperatively on a team, and use the social environment as a backdrop to distinguish themselves as individuals. They express their heart energy by being so completely immersed in their social activities that they "leave behind" the overt emotionality of the Two. It's for this reason that they can be hard to recognize as Heart types.

Type 4 (synthesizing). Fours combine and synthesize aspects of Two and Three within themselves. Like Threes, they immerse themselves deeply into whatever they're doing; like Twos, they consciously feel the flow of their own emotions. The result is a type that is deeply involved in the exploration and synthesis of the feeling world.

Head Types (impersonal, cerebral, knowledge-oriented)

Type 5 (expressive). As a type just entering the Head Center, Fives overtly express the mental energy of this center. They're therefore hard to miss as Head types, in that they tend to be very focused on ideas, systems, theories, and analytical schemes.

Type 6 (receptive). Because Sixes have the ability to receptively attune to what is happening on the subtler levels of life, their understanding of the world around them is informed by inner sensing, not just logic. This can make them more emotionally reactive than Fives and harder to recognize as Head types. But it can also give them a kind of subtle mental radar that tunes them in to unseen dimensions of knowing.

Type 7 (synthesizing). Sevens have the task of "wrapping up" the Head Center by synthesizing the analytical logic of Five and the intuitive sensing of Six in a way that does justice to both ways of knowing. They tend to have an androgynous sense about them and a quickness which is mental in orientation but intuitive in "feel."

The chart below lists more attributes associated with each type according to its *center* and the *role it plays* within that center.

Type by Energy Center & Role Within the Center

	EXPRESSIVE	RECEPTIVE	SYNTHESIZING
Body	**TYPE 8** magnetic, assertive, powerful, grounded, explosive, direct, blunt, decisive	**TYPE 9** open, mild, harmonizing, pacifying, sensible, accepting, habitual, natural	**TYPE 1** fiery, refining, constraining, purifying, sublimating, reforming, idealistic
Heart	**TYPE 2** friendly, emotional, sympathetic, supportive, nurturing, beseeching, advising	**TYPE 3** responsive, communicative, adaptable, resourceful, organized, cooperative	**TYPE 4** introspective, complex, creative, original, yearning, moody, seeking
Head	**TYPE 5** detached, intellectual, systematizing, reflective, analytical, observing, discerning	**TYPE 6** sensitive, perceptive, apprehensive, careful, cautious, protective, watchful, antsy	**TYPE 7** quick, witty, airy, inspired, networking, scattered, futuristic, lively, imaginative

Enneagram Patterns

Chapter 1 provided an overview of the enneagram and the nine types; Chapter 2 focused on each of the types without regard to context. In this chapter, we looked at a simple but powerful way to group the types—as members of one of three energy centers that play a decisive role in shaping our lives. In that sense, we can view the centers as three "meta-types."

While the types can be grouped into triads (groups of three) in many ways, grouping them by energy center is probably the most fundamental triadic grouping. That's why it's a good place to start any deeper exploration of enneagram triadic patterns.

Connecting Points

On the enneagram, the nine points of view are connected by the round ring of the outer circle. But they're also connected by the straight lines that crisscross the middle of the circle in various directions:

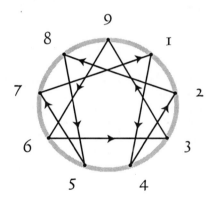

If we take a look at each point on the circle, we see that it's linked via straight lines to exactly two other points on the circle. These are known (no surprise) as its **connecting points**. In this chapter, we're going to look at how each point of view is affected by these two connecting points.

How the Connections Work

If we think of our enneagram type as both an energy resource and a source of motivation, we can think of the connecting points as backup resources that offer additional support for tackling the lessons of life. They're like *fallback* or *go to* positions that provide us with alternative strategies, roles, and perspectives when our usual type-related strategies don't seem adequate for addressing some problem or concern. For example, an Eight parent may find it useful to tap into the nurturing energy of Two (one of Eight's two connecting points) when dealing with small children. Or a One may have a more relaxing vacation if he discovers a way to access the exuberant energy of his connecting point of Seven. Or a Three manager may be less likely to act rashly if he allows his connection to Six to inform his decisions.

Although the connecting points are intended to be secondary resources, it's possible for us to rely quite heavily upon them at times. A common situation where this might happen is when the type-based role somebody would normally assume is already "taken." For example, in a family with several kids, there's a good chance that more than one child will be the same type. Suppose the oldest and youngest are both Sevens. By the time the younger child is born, the older Seven has probably assumed some kind of Sevenish role already (for example, Entertainer or Optimist). In that case, the younger child might take on the One-ish role of Perfecter (becoming serious and precise) or the Five-ish role of Puzzle-Solver (becoming intellectual and self-contained).

The point is that when we need to move away from our customary (type-related) point of view, it's often easiest to move toward one of our connecting points. Alternatively, we can move towards one of our wings (the points on either side).

Often, looking to the wings for support works well when we can stay situated in our type but need to modify our behavior slightly to achieve our goals. For example, a Five who needs to teach a class can "lean into" his Six wing to give him the sense of group solidarity that will help him overcome his natural shyness. But if he needs to become an authority figure that can take charge of an unruly class, he might need to go to his connecting point of Eight, drawing from within himself the gut power and groundedness necessary to restore order. Or he might use the energy of his connecting point of Seven to charm his students into compliance.

Drawing energy from one of our connecting points tends to require more effort—and more of a visible shift—than drawing energy from our wings. When we access the energy of either connecting point, other people observing us may feel like they're seeing a part of us that they've never seen before. It can almost seem like an alternative persona.

Whenever we're "pushed out of" our own point of view because
of our circumstances in life, there's a fair chance that we'll slip into
the point of view of one of our connecting points. In enneagram
lingo, we speak of "going" to that point of view, saying for example,
"Seven goes to One," or "Four goes to Two." We don't actually go
anywhere in the literal sense, because we still have our own point of
view. And no matter how much we "visit" another point of view,
we never completely relinquish our own. At most, we take on a role
heavily informed by the other point of view—but the underlying motivation still arises from our own point of view, not the one we're
"visiting."

Of course, if we have to "visit" for a long time (for example,
because we've taken on a long-term role within our immediate family), we can get so used to our alternative persona that we lose touch
with our own point of view. I know, because this happened to me.
Although I'm a Four, I found it hard to settle into the Four point
of view because it didn't fit with my family situation. So I wound up
taking on the role of one of my connecting points, Point 2, for many
years. I became warm, engaging, and heavily invested in social relationships. This helped me develop friendships and gain skill in social
situations. At the same time, because I'm not a real Two, I sometimes
overplayed the role, becoming overly friendly, oversolicitous, or even
overbearing. At times, I felt like an actor in a Grade-B movie—a caricature instead of a real character.

An actual Two might have some of the problematic tendencies
I had, but she would have better resources to deal with them. I have
resources, too, but most of them are designed to support my "home"
point of view of Four. Since I wasn't living from that point of view,
the Four strategies I might have used weren't really available to me.

I lived as a Two for quite a few years. While it helped me make
friends and gain social confidence, it also created confusion that I
had to sort out later, because I lost track of parts of myself that were
central to my identity. After I shed my Two persona, I began to feel
more like myself. Now I can draw upon the Two energy when it's
useful (for example, in social situations), but I do it in a more natural,
less forced way. By accepting myself as a Four, I can still draw support
from Point 2. But I can more easily access the resources of Point 1,

my other connecting point. The added dimension of One gives me more appreciation for the ethical aspects of life and an understanding of how to express my emotions in a disciplined way.

So when we see people who don't appear to be themselves—who seem more like a caricature than a person—we might ask ourselves whether they might be playing a role associated with a connecting point, especially if their persona seems especially sketchy, thin, or false. (The same scenario can also arise for someone playing a persona associated with their own type, of course. But in that case, the persona is usually better developed and more convincing—the persona seems more like an exaggerated version of something real than a total caricature.)

So far we've been talking about the connecting points as aspects of our own inner psyche. And indeed they are, because each of us has all nine enneagram energies within us to one degree or another. However, we most commonly look at the enneagram as representing nine different personality types. In this case, the connecting points show us typical ways that different types of people relate to one another.

It's common for people who "share a common line" (for example, Twos and Fours, Nines and Threes, or Fives and Eights) to have some sort of natural affinity. When we meet people whose type is one of our connecting points, we may feel as though we already know them. Sometimes the connection is positive; sometimes it's not. In any event, it's useful to realize that there's a reason for this sense of connectedness. Both parties can benefit from understanding the energy dynamics of the situation.

It's also common for people who share no common line to have a somewhat harder time establishing a viable relationship, especially if they're not wing (neighboring) types. If we take the example of a Six, the wing types are Five and Seven and the connecting points are Three and Nine. This leaves four other types with whom the Six has a less direct connection: Types One, Two, Four, and Eight. A Six trying to establish a relationship with individuals of those types may have to work a little harder to find common ground (and vice-versa).

The Direction of the Arrows

As we can see by the diagram on the first page of this chapter, we can reach each of the connecting points either by moving in the same direction as the arrows of energy flow or in the opposite direction. For example, from Point 2, we can either move *with* the arrows to Point 8 or *against* the arrows to Point 4.

So what is the significance, if any, of moving with or against the arrows? It all depends on who you ask. Some people believe that the direction of the arrows has no special significance. Others believe that moving with the arrows is moving in the direction of **disintegration** (pathology) while moving against the arrows is moving in the direction of **integration** (health). The point to which we move in disintegration is often called the *stress point*; the point to which we move in integration is called the *security point* (see the example on the following page).

The direction of the arrows does seem to matter to me; I find I have an easier time accessing the energies of Point 2 (my stress point) than Point 1 (my security point). It feels like the difference between going downhill and uphill. At the same time, I feel more in balance when I make the effort to develop the energies of Point 1.

This is my personal impression. But I've talked to a number of people who say they find it equally easy to access either connecting point—and who don't see either point as more advantageous than the other, in terms of its positive vs. negative effects. So the jury is still out on this question.

Why Study the Connections?

The advantage of studying the connecting points is that we're able to avail ourselves of their resources in a conscious way, as opposed to "falling" into their energetic patterns without intending to. In the latter case, we tend to unconsciously take on characteristics of either connecting point as opposed to doing so in a way that allows us to be more self-aware and discriminating.

Another advantage is that understanding the connecting points enables us to better type ourselves and other people, because we begin to see each type in the context of its connecting points. With experience, it's possible to pinpoint someone's type by noticing

Stress point

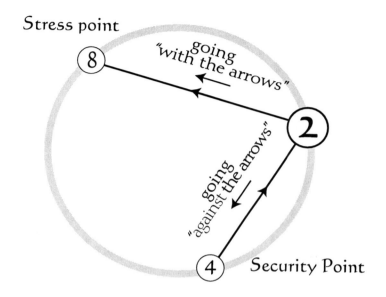

"with going
the arrows"

"going
against the arrows"

Security Point

Moving With or Against the Arrows

not only his type energy, but the "energetic overtones" of the connecting points.

So suppose I'm not sure whether someone is a Nine or Five. (Maybe he's fairly impassive and non-judgmental.) I can look not only at the Nine and Five type descriptions but at the descriptions of his potential connecting points, to see which ones are the best match.

Does he have a tendency to become anxious under stress (9 ▶ 6) and to sometimes work without stopping (9 ▶ 3)? Or does he become easily fascinated with idealistic ideas (5 ▶ 7) and emphatic about his opinions (5 ▶ 8)? With practice, it becomes possible to see each type as a constellation of energies informed not only by the type energy, but by the energies of its connecting points.

The following section describes the relationship between each point and its two connecting points.

ONE connects to Four and Seven.

Connection to Seven. The connection to Seven brings Ones a greater ability to relax and let down their hair. They become more joyful, care-free, and innovative and less rule-bound and strict about regulating every aspect of their lives. They discover the ability to play and enjoy everyday activities. However, the heady energy of Seven can be intoxicating to Ones, who can get carried away by the sense of unaccustomed freedom. So they need to learn how to appreciate this energy (rather than disapprove of it), but to temper their appreciation with good judgment.

Connection to Four. This connection brings greater awareness of their interiority, especially their feelings, which helps Ones get in touch with their humanity and originality. Then they can move beyond the two-dimensional black and white thinking that tempts them to reduce everything in life to a "right vs. wrong" proposition. This connection also allows them access to their artistic and literary talents, which brings inner enrichment to their lives. But it can also bring moodiness, as they become more acutely aware of the difference between how they actually feel and how they believe they *ought* to feel. This conflict can make them uncomfortable and tense, especially if they're determined to stave off unacceptable emotions. The antidote is to tamp down the "oughts" and gracefully accept their emotions for what they really are.

Comments. Points 1, 4, and 7 are all restive, idealistic types that like to think up new ideas and initiate new projects. As gut types, Ones are in an excellent position to ground this idealism, so it becomes channeled in a practical yet principled way. The energy of Seven takes them up into the sky while the energy of Four takes them down into the depths. What Ones need to do is learn how to stay firmly rooted in the earth, but allow themselves to stretch in both directions (without censoring the experience). When they're able to open up, they retain the principled approach of their type but gain the flexibility and inspiration of the Seven and the imagination and soulfulness of the Four.

TWO connects to Four and Eight.

Connection to Four. This connection enables the Two to get in touch with the deeper emotions and motivations that underlie her shifting emotionality, which gives her a clearer sense of who she really is when she looks beyond the image she cultivates. 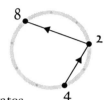 She gains a better understanding of the dynamics involved in her relationships and the ability to interact with others from a deeper, more introspective place within herself. But the move from Two to Four can be initially painful for a Two, because it forces her to see through surface emotions and really "own" her core motivations (take responsibility for them). It's better if she does this consciously; if she unconsciously "falls" to Four, she's likely to become intensely emotional and self-dramatizing.

Connection to Eight. When the Two goes to Eight, she learns to speak up for herself—to be direct and assertive—so that she doesn't have to seek what she needs by emotional manipulation. The Eight energy has the potential to ground her emotions, bolster her self-confidence, and help her tap into her sense of personal honor, so she's able to feel good about acting independently. At the same time, the move to Eight can bring sudden surges of aggression, possessiveness, and a domineering tendency which can create archetypes like the Devouring Mother or the Avenging Angel. So Twos can benefit from cultivating the kind of self-discipline that enables them to use the powerful Eight energy with self-control.

Comments. Twos are heart types who can get so caught up in the surface-level flow of their emotions that they lose their sense of identity in the process. From Point 8, they gain the ability to be less personally reactive and more grounded; from Point 4, they gain the ability to get in touch with their innermost sense of self. These resources can help them feel steadier and more in charge, so they stop identifying with every passing emotion. Both connections potentially help them give more deeply from the heart—and with no strings attached!

THREE connects to Six and Nine.

Connection to Six. Threes are outgoing and ready to act; they tend to take a proactive stance, whatever the situation. Connecting to Six slows them down and helps them be more cautious, so they avoid acting unwisely or prematurely. It also helps them consider the effects of their actions on other people, especially those they love. For achievement-oriented Threes, this is important, because it can be difficult for them to remember other people's needs when making plans. At Point 6, the Three becomes more aware of the surrounding environment (and the people who populate it). This is a positive development, just so long as the Three doesn't allow this awareness to create anxiety and the tendency to second-guess.

Connection to Nine. Threes have such a busy energy that they find it hard to slow down. Point 9 gives them a place where they can kick back, relax, and let go of the cares of the day. The only problem for Threes is that they tend to get *so* busy that by the time they tap into their more mellow Nine energy, they're often far past the point where they can actually enjoy its benefits. When that happens, they either keep working in a zoned-out state or collapse into a puddle, unable to do much at all. So their challenge is to learn how to access the steady Nine energy in a balanced way, so that they can work without rushing and can relax without collapsing.

Comments. Points 3-6-9 form the inner triangle of the enneagram. So each of these three points acts as a connecting point for the other two. Types 3, 6, and 9 are often said to move more easily "along the lines" (to their connecting points) than the other six types. They all know how to adapt, but each adapts to achieve different purposes. Point 3 adapts in order to excel, Point 6 adapts in order to serve and preserve, and Point 9 adapts in order to participate with others. When the Three moves to Six, he takes on a more service-oriented role; he can excel at service or serve by excelling. When the Three moves to Nine, he can begin to learn how to "slow down and smell the roses," participating in life not just to win but to experience the joy of being alive.

FOUR connects to One and Two.

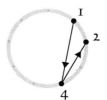

Connection to One. The energy at Four is intense, dramatic, and potentiating. It's hard to contain and seeks expression in artistic projects of all kinds. The connection to One creates the opportunity for disciplining this restless energy, so that it's subject to the kind of control needed for cultivated expression. The result is a way of working that is one-pointed, refined, and subjectively satisfying. However, given the Four's penchant for excess, it's important for her to allow the grounding properties of One to curb her natural inclination to go to emotional extremes, especially when working on creative projects or causes for which she has a passion. This connection can also bring out the One-ish tendency to become resentful or critical.

Connection to Two. The Two energy is warm, friendly, and sympathetic, and it helps the Four to gain a mellower, more compassionate outlook on life. It also helps her find common ground with other people and establish closer social ties. At the same time, too much Two energy can amp up her emotions, making it hard to achieve emotional balance. It can initiate the kind of emotional downward spiral where unsatisfied yearning leads to self-pity, self-pity leads to isolation, and isolation leads to depression. Fours already have a lot of emotional energy; the added energy from Two can make for a pretty soggy, heavy load unless the Four learns how to temper emotionality with objectivity.

Comments. The challenge at Four is to use the energy of the other two connecting points in a way that helps her balance her emotions and curb her tendency to become moody and self-absorbed. Fours are good at creative expression but often find it difficult to adjust to the needs of other people or to the requirements of conventional social situations. Both of their connecting points offer support in this area: Point 1 shows Fours how to keep their emotions in check and gain self-control; Point 2 enables them to open their hearts and reach out to others. They can draw upon both of these resources to escape the trap of loneliness and isolation.

FIVE connects to Eight and Seven.

Connection to Eight. Five is the most introverted of types while Eight is the opposite—at
least in appearance. The connection between Five
and Eight gives the Five access to the kind of "big"
energy that can help him stand his ground, even
when he doesn't say much. At Point 5, the Eight energy
gets introverted and focused, creating an energy potential that's like
the power of the atom—very compact and intense. But because it's
so introverted, we usually see it only indirectly, in the creative insights of the Five's intellect. On the rare occasions when the Five
loses control of this energy (that is, when he gets angry), the result-
ing explosion can startle even an Eight.

Connection to Seven. The Seven connection gives Fives access
to an imaginative, childlike energy that they can use to turn work into
play. But in a Five, the Seven energy tends to be closely-held, and it
is often expressed in subtle ways. But let a small child come along
and a remarkable transformation takes place. The usually reticent
Five becomes the most wonderful playmate imaginable, happily as-
sembling toy trains, doing magic tricks, or giving piggyback rides.
The Seven connection also gives Fives a love for more grown-up
games and puzzles. Once a Five finds a game he really likes (such as
chess, fantasy role playing, or computer games), he'll play for hours
(or even days) on end. Fives can get so sucked into fascinating activities that it's hard to break away, so they need to learn how to balance
fantasy with reality.

Comments. Fives are drawn inward and downward, into the
creative core of life. Like Fours, Fives have the kind of connection
with the upper points in the enneagram (in this case, Points 7 and 8)
that's designed to help them achieve a balance between their inner
and outer lives. But they have to use that opportunity in a way that
supports balance and integration. If the Four's 1-2-4 combination
gives them access to discipline, empathy, and creativity, the Five's
5-7-8 combination gives them access to intellect, playfulness, and
power. The challenge for Fives is to harness their unusual combination of assets in a way that allows them to be creative, but that
retains the human touch.

SIX connects to Nine and Three.

Connection to Nine. Six is the place of apprehension, both in the cognitive and emotional sense.
The connection to Nine can serve as a source of
calm in the eye of the storm. The greatest difficulty
at Six is the lack of any firm ground on which to stand;
Nine potentially provides that grounding. The Nine energy reminds
the Six that although life may look dangerous and unpredictable,
there's always an inner sanctuary in which she can rest. At Nine, she
can become more present and open to the energy of the moment,
instead of being caught up in worries about the future or habits of
the past. But she needs to take care that she doesn't use the Nine
energy to zone out, flee from anxiety, or put off scary decisions.

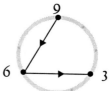

Connection to Three. When Sixes go to Three, it tends to amp
up their already amped-up energy—it can really wind them up and
get them going. The only questions is, Where? The combined influence of Sixish apprehension with Three-ish aspiration can push a
Six to act too quickly, without exercising good judgment, especially
if she's already jumpy. So it's important for the Six to be aware of
what's motivating her—to make sure that she doesn't get so carried away that she loses her discernment and inner poise. For the
balanced Six, the move to Three can result in high achievement,
because of her service ethic and willingness to work hard.

Comments. At Point 6 on the enneagram, individuals becoming extremely sensitive to what's going on in the outer environment.
It's a place of great volatility. However, it has great transformational
potential, because the flip side of volatility is the ability to experience
positive transformational change. But such change can only happen
to the extent that the Six is able to ground herself and transform her
anxiety into action. Each connecting point gives her a tool for that
purpose. Point 9 brings a sense of connectedness to the earth and
inner calm; Point 3 provides an opportunity for outer achievement
and development. The energy of both these connecting points gives
the Six resources she can use to quell her fear and transform doubt
into resolve.

SEVEN connects to Five and One.

Connection to Five. In the first half of their lives, Sevens are typically so high-energy and action-oriented that they may not realize that Five is a resource from which they can draw. This situation tends to persist until they encounter a solid obstacle that slows them down (like advancing age). The energy of Five is much slower, so it can act as a "brake" for the impetuousness of the Seven—once the Seven is actually willing to slow down. The need to slow down is a tough thing for a Seven to accept, because his greatest pleasure is the sensation of boundless freedom. But the need for freedom can potentially lead the Seven into impulsive decisions that may actually result in a loss of freedom. The Five energy can help the Seven become steadier, less hyperactive, and more mature.

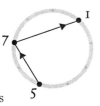

Connection to One. This connection brings greater detail-orientation and discipline, as well as the ability to follow through on decisions. But when Sevens try to assimilate the energy of Point 1, they often take on a certain prim and proper attitude that seems a bit strange when grafted onto to the normally buoyant Seven personality. At Point 1, Sevens get "clean and sober" (at least temporarily). They also tend to get more critical than usual (both in a positive and negative sense). They're also more likely to get caught up in revolutionary ideals or causes, because while both Sevens and Ones are idealistic, Ones have a particularly deep sense of moral conviction and the determination to fight for their ideals. Integrating the strictly contained energy of One with the optimism of Seven is not all that easy, but it can potentially ground the Seven and help him maintain focus.

Comments. Seven is the energy we'd all like to have: the energy of youth, joy, and freedom. But without a sense of proportion, these positive traits can easily turn into negatives: immaturity, irresponsibility, and the inability to commit. The energy of the connecting points can mitigate these tendencies. The Five energy can help the Seven slow down, consider his options, and make more rational decisions. The One energy can help him cultivate excellence, an eye for detail, and the ability to translate ideas into action.

EIGHT connects to Two and Five.

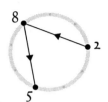

Connection to Two. Eights are natural leaders who tend to see themselves as the standard by which all else is measured. The connection to Two gives them the ability to get in touch with their emotional vulnerability and to develop greater empathy for others, enabling them to lead with their heart, not just their gut. It helps them channel the humanitarian energy of Two into practical projects that can help transform the world, often on a grand scale. But this kind of achievement demands the ability to exercise self-control and to avoid taking things too personally. If Eights can't or won't develop it, the connection to Two can exaggerate their tendency to see themselves as the target of everybody else's aggression (which will in turn allow them to justify their own aggressive urges).

Connection to Five. The connection to Five gives the physically-active Eight the ability to withdraw into herself, get quiet, and regroup. Eights need this opportunity, especially when they become emotionally wounded or overwhelmed. They need the chance to go into "neutral," so they can let pent-up emotional energies slowly drain away. When they take advantage of this opportunity, they gain the mental clarity, detachment, and impartiality they need to exercise power in a way that befits a real leader. Of course, it can be hard for the big, blustery Eight to move into the Five space, because it can seem like a forced retreat into unfamiliar territory. If the Eight is not careful, this time of withdrawal can become a time for incubating grudges or building up negative thoughts.

Comments. A big challenge for Eights is to discover that they are both more *and* less than they appear to be. On one hand, they see themselves as all-encompassing in a way that is hard for other types to imagine; this innate sense of Self (with the capital "S") gives rise to a natural dominance that we don't see in other types. On the other hand, Eights have a painfully shy side, especially when life plops them out of their comfort zone. Both of their connection points provide them with ways to come to terms with these two sides of themselves. Point 2 helps them find their hearts while Point 5 helps them acquire a cooler, more thoughtful outlook on life.

NINE connects to Three and Six.

Connection to Three. Nines typically have a hard time getting things done—not because they're lazy but because they're slow starters who are easily distracted. The connection to Three helps them get moving and stay on track. They become focused, organized, and goal-oriented. But this connection can also give them the Three-ish tendency to go without stopping—forgetting to eat, rest, or exercise. Once they get into a certain groove, they can be almost as capable as Threes of exhausting themselves with work. To work effectively, they need some sort of concrete plan that helps them organize their activities and reminds them when it's time to do something else.

Connection to Six. The Six energy can be "edgy" and destabilizing to a Nine. However, this very edginess may be helpful to the stolid Nine who tends to hang back, wanting to stay too much in the groove of his usual routine. The Six energy pokes and prods at the Nine to respond, which is sometimes exactly what the Nine needs to get over the tendency to distract himself with little things in the surrounding environment (and thus avoid focusing on his own personal needs and desires). If the Nine is receptive, he can use this Six energy to gain the oomph to take on his own inner resistance. Otherwise, the energy will tend to "sit on him," making him anxious and worried until he's willing to confront his natural stubbornness and reluctance to change.

Comments. Nines are usually kind, receptive, and unassuming individuals who make good friends and responsible workers. They tend to have diverse interests and many friends. There's only one thing missing: a tangible sense of who they actually are as individuals. So the challenge for a Nine is getting motivated enough to explore his inner self. From Point 3, he gains a sense of motivation and the ability to get going; from Point 6, he gets the edge he needs to cut through his avoidance of introspection. Both energies are helpful for the Nine who's striving to overcome confusion and gain inner clarity about the nature of his unique gifts, hopes, and dreams.

− 5 −
Subtype Arenas

The enneagram subtypes are one of the most interesting areas of enneagram study. The first time I attended an enneagram event, I walked into a workshop on enneagram subtypes and I've been hooked ever since.

Basically, the subtype approach starts with the idea that there are three main arenas within which people operate—the arena of the self, the arena of sexuality, and the arena of the social world:

We can look at how each of the nine types shows up in each of these three subtype arenas:

Alternatively, we can generate three profiles for each enneagram type, one for each arena (SP = self-preservation arena, SX = sexual arena, SOC = social arena). Once we know our type, we can read a description of these subtype profiles to determine which subtype arena is most influential:

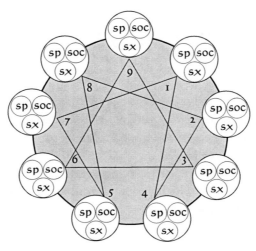

Chapter 6 provides profiles of all 27 subtypes (nine types × three subtype arenas). But this information is more useful once we already have some understanding of the subtype arenas independent of the enneagram types. So that's what I'll discuss in the rest of this chapter, starting with what makes my approach to the subtypes unique.

My Take on the Subtypes

The most popular theory regarding the enneagram subtypes is based on the assumption that they're instinctual in nature. That's why they're termed either *instinctual subtypes* (by Claudio Naranjo and many others) or *instinctual variants* (by Don Riso and Russ Hudson). As Naranjo notes on p. 9 of his book *Character and Neurosis*, "the theory proposed here acknowledges three basic instincts and goals behind the multiplicity of human motivation (purely spiritual motivation excluded): survival, pleasure, and relationship."

The three motivations he delineates correspond exactly to the three subtype arenas of self-preservation, sexuality, and sociability.

So what Naranjo is claiming here is that our actions in these three arenas of human activity are mainly motivated by biologically-based, instinctually-motivated drives. Elsewhere, he characterizes the motivations of these drives as deficiency-based. While he speaks of the possibility that a person may be motivated by some kind of spiritual impulse (which is presumably *not* a form of deficiency motivation), he never says a word about the nature of this spiritual motivation or how it might be distinguished from deficiency motivation.

Despite its brevity, this passage offers a good description of the theory which underlies the idea that the subtypes are instinctual in nature, a theory that is psychoanalytic in origin. It's also a theory based on a pretty reductionistic view of human nature. If we accept its premises, we're almost inevitably forced to accept the idea that actions which appear to be altruistic, innovative, or ethical are actually motivated by primitive impulses arising out of a turbulent and unredeemed *id* whose drives are unavoidably atavistic (selfish) in nature. We might think we're acting out of some noble and unselfish impulse, but if we do, we're almost certainly deluding ourselves.

That's the theory in a nutshell. But I don't buy it. I see our core motivation as arising from our type; as such, our core motivation is archetypal (spiritual) in nature. I see the instincts as primal energies designed to support life on the physical plane (by giving us the bodily intelligence we need to survive in a physical vehicle). While instincts can be said to possess motivation of a sort, this motivation is subordinate to the motivation of the psyche or soul-self. Simply put, we are "spiritual beings having a human experience."

Thus, I do not view the three subtype arenas as instinctual in nature. I view them simply as three diverse arenas for human action. When combined with the nine types, they can generate 27 personality profiles that describe how each type tends to act in each arena. I use these subtype profiles as the basis for much of my enneagram work because they are much richer in detail than generic type descriptions.

There's more that could be said about the subtypes from a theoretical point of view, but my focus here is simply to introduce a new way of working with them and to briefly explain my reasons for adopting an alternative approach.

Why Aren't the Subtypes Better Understood?

The enneagram subtypes are less well-known than the nine types, despite the fact that the subtype teachings have been around for many years. I see four main reasons for this lack of familiarity.

First, if we consider the subtypes to be instinctual and the types to be fixated, then the subtype descriptions become 27 profiles of fixation in action. It's bad enough studying nine ways that people get stuck; who wants to know 27? As long as type and subtype are seen as ways to describe human failings, there's going to be a limited amount of interest in acquiring a detailed understanding of those failings.

Second, there are 27 subtypes—that's a lot of profiles, a lot of information to remember! It's not easy to devise teaching methods that enable people to remember the subtypes, especially in a one- or two-day workshop.

Third, there is little published on the subtypes, except in *Enneagram Monthly* articles or in the form of bound xeroxed sheets that have limited distribution.

Fourth, the terminology used to describe the subtypes can be confusing. As I mentioned earlier, some people call them *instinctual subtypes*; others call them *instinctual variants*. In addition, some teachers (Riso and Hudson) refer to the wing types as *subtypes*. In addition, there's no way to talk about the subtype arenas independently of the subtype profiles (please see my comment below).

Despite these barriers to understanding, the subtypes are well worth discovering, because they have the potential to provide us with a much more nuanced understanding of the types.

Two notes: First, the term *subtype arena* is my invention. I created it in order to discuss the subtypes independently of type. There's no existing term for this purpose, so it was necessary to devise one. Second, I'm not a big fan of the term *self-preservation subtype*, which is how the arena of the self is usually described. It's too negative; and it's also suggestive of a survival orientation. While this subtype arena does indeed focus on survival, there's a lot more to it than that (see the attributes on the page opposite). However, the term *self-preservation subtype* is so common in enneagram circles that I retain it in order to keep confusion to a minimum. All things being equal, I would prefer calling the self-preservation arena the *arena of the self* (as I did earlier) and to call the self-preservation subtype the *self-responsibility subtype.*

Exploring the Subtype Arenas

As mentioned earlier, we can look at the subtypes from essentially two perspectives. The first perspective enables us to focus our attention on the three subtype arenas in isolation; the second perspective enables us to focus our attention on nine types and how their orientation differs according to which arena they're in. The graphic below reflects the first perspective in that it focuses on each arena without regard to enneagram type. It illustrates the many dimensions of each arena.

The Three Subtype Arenas

self-preservation	sexuality	sociability
home, shelter, family, friends, food, diet, health care, comfort, personal habits, garden, the crops, self-care, caring for others, survival, family support systems, parents, children, ordinary life, work, common sense, personal values, self-reliance, small business, local matters, independence, individuality, ingenuity, the soil, the earth	creativity, sexuality, sensuality, dreams, visions, mysticism, union, spiritual awakening, artistic inspiration, shared values, competition, aspiration, inspiration, originality, imagination, myths & legends, dreams, drama, kundalini, sin & redemption, taboos, initiation rituals & rites of passage, alchemy, magic, heaven & hell, the underworld	neighbors, community, public areas, government, laws, courts, institutions, organizations, companies, culture, race relations, ethical systems, manners, humanitarian projects, politics, systems theory, social activism, dharma, in-group/out-group dynamics, social status, prestige, duty, games, socializing, gangs, the military, the world

"Self-preservation" is not just about survival—it's about self-hood, individuality, personal values, health, family, and our immediate environment. "Sexuality" is not just about sex—it's about creativity, originality, mysticism, spirituality, Shadow issues, and artistic inspiration. And "sociability" isn't just about being in a group—it's about law, culture, shared responsibility, politics, government, systems, and the fulfillment of dharma. (With all these dimensions for each sub-type, can you see why I find it hard to see them as expressions of instinct, and nothing more?)

I like to use this arena-oriented approach for introducing the sub-types because it makes them memorable (in that it initially focuses on just three categories, not 27). Once we're comfortable with three are-nas, it's not hard to understand how type motivation might influence our actions in each arena. We can determine our dominant arena and use this information to generate a finer-grained type profile. If we take Type 9 as an example, we can generate brief profiles for three kinds of Nines: Self-preservation Nines, Sexual Nines, and Social Nines. If we do, we learn that

- Self-preservation (SP) Nines tend to be homebodies who like the simple pleasures of life
- Sexual (SX) Nines seek a partner with whom to merge and often have a mystical or devotional streak
- Social (SOC) Nines particularly enjoy blending into groups

Although all Nines will probably identify somewhat with each profile, they will probably identify with one of them most strongly. This is their dominant subtype.

The next chapter presents longer profiles for each subtype; Appendix C presents a subtypes test to help you determine your dominant subtype arena.

Determining Your Subtype Arena

In the Riso-Hudson approach to the enneagram, there's an effort made to determine the "stacking order" of the subtypes, that is, which arena is most dominant, second most dominant, and least dominant. This adds another layer of refinement to the typing process.

I've used this idea as the basis for developing six subtype profiles that are independent of type:

- self-preservation subtype
- sexual subtype
- social subtype
- self-preservation/sexual subtype
- self-preservation/social subtype
- sexual/social subtype

Again, using Type 9 as an example, we could have six kinds of Nines: three with one dominant subtype arena (SP, SX, or SOC) and three others with two dominant arenas (SP-SX, SP-SOC, or SX-SOC).

It's theoretically possible to go further and determine which of the two dominant arenas is *most* dominant. In this case, we'd have one profile for Nines whose subtype is SP-SX and another profile for Nines whose subtype is SX-SP, based on the order of dominance. But such a breakdown is probably too fine-grained to be useful.

The following section offers a brief description of the six possible subtype combinations.

The Subtype Arenas

The Self-Preservation Subtype. An SP individual is the "salt of the earth." He's self-reliant, commonsensical, and very much concerned with his immediate environment—his home, family, and close friends. He's good with money, seldom going into debt; if he does incur debts, he repays them as promptly as possible. He values personal comfort over glamour, and as a rule, he's not terribly charismatic. He likes to do work that enables him to be independent; by the same token, he'd generally rather work alone than have to direct others (or be directed by a manager). An SP person adjusts well to the demands of the physical world; he seldom indulges in flights of fancy. He believes in personal responsibility and has little tolerance for people who are flighty, irresponsible, or dishonest. He dislikes phonies and is not easily flattered by false compliments. His manner tends to be direct rather than diplomatic, but the gruff exterior often conceals a heart of gold. He can be very patient and calm, and usually makes an excellent parent. At the same time, change can be hard for him, especially quick change. He can also be too serious and inflexible at times—a real stick-in-the-mud. So he would do well to cultivate flexibility, tolerance, and a sense of humor.

Sexual Subtype. I suppose we could call this the "exciting" subtype, in that SX persons tend to be sexy, charismatic, creative, mystical, sacrificial, and seductive (although not all of these qualities are usually present in a single individual!). When we talk about sexuality in the context of the subtypes, the discussion includes not only intimacy and sexual activity but mysticism and creativity. The individual of this subtype tends to be intense, charismatic, and high-energy. She attracts attention wherever she goes. She has the ability to inspire others and elicit their help, especially in a one-to-one situation. She's imaginative and entertaining, and she often has a great sense of humor. She can often charm her way out of dicey situations, which obviously makes it tempting to overuse this talent. This subtype is extremely dynamic, and the same dynamism that makes SX subtypes charismatic also makes it hard for them to stick with anything long enough to get something accomplished. Likewise, intimate relationships can be intensely involving in the short-term, but hard to sustain (because SX subtypes often prefer the process of falling in love to the work of building a long-term relationship). To be balanced, an SX subtype typically needs to develop the kind of good habits, self-control, and discipline that will give her the balance she needs to create a life that has a solid foundation.

Social Subtype. The focus here is on the group and how individuals relate to it. So the SOC person is attracted to the arena of the community, the state, and the nation—even the entire world. He's interested in the processes by which groups develop, and he's attracted to work that allows him some kind of participatory, facilitative, or leadership role. Generally speaking, he'd prefer to play a smaller role within a group than a larger role outside of it. An individual with a heavy social emphasis is often attracted to a partner who's involved in the same group or who likes the same kind of social activities. He may be particularly sensitive to the demands of the family or society when choosing this partner. He gains energy from group work and enjoys participating in group processes. Sensitive to power shifts and in-group/out-group dynamics, he knows how to skillfully navigate the currents of an organization. He values group loyalty and would find it difficult to stand against any group that means a lot to him. But he can usually manage to avoid such a fate due to his sensitivity to group norms and his diplomatic ability. He tends to see group values (such as service or social responsibility) as more important than individual values, and he's often attracted to activities designed to further some sort of social, cultural, or humanitarian goal. He tends to be outgoing, but is usually adept at curbing his emotions in order to avoid disrupting the group. However, if he's not careful, he can get so identified with the group that he loses touch with his own personal values and individual sense of humanity.

Self-preservation/Sexual Subtype. When both these arenas are influential, we have an individual who combines the practical-ity of the self-preservation subtype with the intensity and creative impulses of the sexual subtype. This can make for a creative person with the "push" to get their projects done, projects that tend to be autobiographical or intimately tied to personal concerns. An SP-SX individual tends to be passionate about the positions she takes and is willing to stand up for her principles. She likes to work alone or with one special partner rather than a group. She's also a self-starter who tends to do things her own way. Although she likes the inten-sity of an intimate relationship, she never completely gives herself away for the sake of intimacy. But once she finds someone to love, she'll try hard to make the relationship work. She also likes to just hang out, but with a single friend or two, not a crowd. She likes to take care of business (pay bills, etc.) but also doesn't like to be dis-tracted from more interesting, creative pursuits, so she's apt to try to get the responsible stuff over with quickly so she can get back to the interesting and creative activities that she really enjoys.

Self-preservation/Social Subtype. Restrained, modest, and cooperative in nature, an SP-SOC individual combines a sense of personal responsibility with a keen interest in civic affairs. Because of his groundedness and work ethic, he's an excellent team member and will work steadily to fulfill whatever responsibilities he takes on. He finds conflict distasteful and does what he can to avoid it. As a result, if he *does* gets involved in any sort of social change effort, he's more likely to be collecting petitions than manning the barricades. Pragmatic and politic, he knows how to pick his battles and when to give tit for tat. Public service work can attract him, because it combines his preference for solid employment with a talent for creating functional social service systems. But he can work either behind the scenes or in the midst of a crowd—what matters is that he is able to serve the group in a concrete way. Because he tends to be less emotional than other subtypes, he can remain calm in the midst of chaotic situations. However, emotional intimacy may be hard to come by, because he can be relatively oblivious to the emotional subtleties that make intimacy possible.

Sexual/Social Subtype. The combination of the intense, sexually-charged energy of the SX profile with the sociable, group-oriented energy of the SOC profile creates a high-energy, charismatic individual who likes to be part of the group scene. The SX-SOC person enjoys keeping up with the latest styles and likes being "in with the in crowd." If she has artistic tastes, they're sure to be in line with current trends; professions that attract her include fashion design, public architecture, the performing arts, and TV journalism. Whatever profession she picks, it's likely to be something in the public eye—something that attracts a wide audience—because solitary work does not appeal. This individual tends to be ambitious and often realizes her ambitions because she not only has drive but also flexibility and an innate ability to align with the will of the group, an ability that cuts both ways. On one hand, it makes her popular with like-minded others. On the other, it can also make her so dependent on the group for grounding that she seems to lack any real substance of her own. Intimate relationships tend to be sought on the twin bases of attraction and prestige; these don't necessarily create the kind of shared intimacy that helps a partnership weather the vicissitudes of life.

– 6 –

Subtype Descriptions

This chapter describes the 27 subtypes (three main subtype arenas × nine types). If you think you have more than one dominant subtype arena (see previous chapter), consult both subtype descriptions for your type and combine them to create a more detailed portrait of yourself.

Enneagram Subtypes

Point	SELF-PRESERVATION ARENA (focus is on the self, bodily integrity & the home)	SEXUAL ARENA (focus is on intimacy, creativity, aspiration & intensity)	SOCIAL ARENA (focus is on the group, community & society)
1	Detailer	Crusader	Lawmaker
2	Matriarch	Romantic	Diplomat
3	Pragmatist	Superstar	Politician
4	Artisan	Dramatist	Social Critic
5	Archivist	Wizard	Professor
6	Family Preserver	Scrapper	Guardian
7	Bon Vivant	Trickster	Visionary
8	Weight Lifter	Knight	Leader
9	Comfort Seeker	Mystic	Cooperator

Self-preservation (SP) Subtypes

All SP subtypes share in common a focus on the self, the immediate surroundings, physical comfort, personal independence, and individual values. They're protective of their space, their homes, and their families, because they have an intuitive awareness of how important it is for people to ground themselves on earth in a very tangible, physical way. They also tend to be socially reserved. But they're usually willing to be drawn out by people they trust. So they appreciate efforts made by others to get to know them.

SP One—The Detailer. *Modest, austere, reserved, self-contained, thrifty, meticulous.* You know the picture *American Gothic* (the one with the farmer, the wife, and the pitchfork in front of a plain farmhouse)? It must have been made with this subtype in mind. SP Ones are the kind of folks that remind us of a bygone era—straight, upright, and principled. They're Shaker-plain (in attitude, not necessarily in looks) and they have a "no-frills" attitude toward life. They're also traditional in their ways but are less family-oriented than some self-preservation subtypes, because of a preference to spend time in solitude. They don't tend to talk much. But when they do, they usually have something substantive to say. They're often successful small business owners, but aren't necessarily all that easy to work for because of their high standards and critical disposition.

self-preservation arena

home, shelter, family, friends, food, diet, health care, comfort, personal habits, garden, the crops, self-care, caring for others, survival, family support systems, parents, children, ordinary life, work, common sense, personal values, self-reliance, small business, local matters, independence, individuality, ingenuity, the soil, the earth

Behind the criticality is a good deal of tension caused by the conflict between their energetic intensity (because they're a fire type) and their natural reserve and desire to keep their own counsel—a tendency that's particularly strong in this One subtype. The other thing that makes them critical is their very real One-ish ability to discriminate between truth and lies. They can spot a phony a mile away, but unlike the other two subtypes, they'll tend to avoid such a person rather than confront him (especially if they have a Nine wing). The main way they uphold their values is to embody them, becoming a living example of what they believe. So this is the subtype that reminds us that old-fashioned values aren't really dead—they're still preserved by these shy but dignified Ones.

If you ever want fine work at fair prices, this is the person to seek. SP Ones make great craftsmen, detail carpenters, instrument makers, or copy editors, because they take pride in their work and make sure that the job is done right. Their idealism and connection to Four often give them an unexpected artistic or inventive streak.

If you can gain their trust, SP Ones make wonderful friends upon whom you can rely. Making friends with them is not always easy, though, because they tend toward shyness and social reticence. And they're naturally suspicious of flattery. So friendship can't be faked, it has to be earned. How? By being honest, straightforward, and upright—just like they are! If you meet their tests, they may be willing to open up and show you that there's more to them than meets the eye. Although they tend to let others make the first move in a friendship, they appreciate the support of people who are more outgoing and relaxed (this helps them to relax, too).

SP Two—The Matriarch. *Strong, competent, "take-charge," nurturing, supportive.* This Two subtype is sometimes called the Nurturer, and there is indeed a lot of nurturing associated with it. But there's a good deal more—which is why I chose the Matriarch for a subtype label. Although this is a term normally applied to females, it's an archetype that can apply to either sex. Male SP Twos are as capable of playing as matriarchal a role as females, if the culture permits it.

In many cultures, the female head of the household has traditionally been required to play the role of an SP Two—to take charge of the family and the home. Families were large and the job was tough, so even females who weren't this type or subtype were expected, upon marriage, to assume this role (unless they had a mother-in-law who was already taking it on).

We still see this image in films showing mothers in traditional families. The mothers in these films are formidable—powerful, dominant (if not domineering), and very sure of themselves and their opinions. They're tough in their defense of the family. And they'll go to great lengths to keep everybody in tow. At the same time, they can be incredibly tender when there's a sick child in the family or an animal that needs rescuing. They're usually versatile, ingenious, and supportive, too.

Of course, not everybody who's an SP Two plays a "mom" role. But the same kind of maternal energy can show up in other venues—in the form of a head nurse, army medic, kindergarten teacher, head cook, or office manager. SP Twos often love to cook—and also to eat. And they love serving food to people who are close to them. They're very much homebodies and like to have people visit them at home.

SP Twos will go out of their way to do things for others, but if they feel unappreciated, they can be self-dramatizing and demanding (which is why this subtype has sometimes been called Me First). If forced to take on a matriarchal role before they're ready, they can become more like a manipulative child than a nurturing parent, even demanding from their own children the nurturing they don't know how to give.

Generally speaking, SP Twos need to be treated with honor and respect but also firmness. They tend to have a "big" energy that needs restraining at times. If they won't do it themselves, those around them need to help them do it by setting limits and refusing to allow the Two to overrun or over-coddle them. When dealing with SP Twos who assume the role of a child, it's helpful to be encouraging but firm, so that they have the kind of support that makes them feel safe but also encourages them to grow up. Only when they gain real maturity can they competently assume the demanding role of Matriarch.

SP Three—The Pragmatist. *Practical, concrete, materially-oriented, competent, accommodating.* All Threes tend to be practical and willing to work hard, but SP Threes are even more hard-driving than other Threes. Like SP Twos, they like to take charge of their immediate environment, but while SP Twos are more focused on the people in the environment (with other things being secondary), SP Threes are more focused on taking charge of the environment itself—on creating a home, office, or garden that represents an ideal of some kind. Since people are part of that environment, they'll be cared for, too. But they're not really the main focus. The focus is more on creating some kind of image—the kind that will give the Three a sense of confidence. Threes are sensitive to current trends, so they're likely to create an image that bows to fashion in some way. Traditionally, an SP Three would be characterized as the "perfect homemaker" or "company man." But nowadays, not too many Threes, either male or female, are hanging around the house (unless they're caring for small children). And the role of the company man is no longer viable in a world where most savvy business people get ahead by changing jobs every 3 – 4 years.

SP Threes are probably the most materially-oriented of all the SP subtypes. It's not because they're especially greedy but because having a solid financial base gives them a sense of security in a world which they see as fast-changing and competitive. It can be hard for SP Threes to get their minds off security issues long enough to focus deeply on relationships—or even to find time for them. If they're not careful, they can get into the habit of objectifying their relationships instead of nourishing them. On the other hand, because they're adaptable, once it's pointed out to them that relationships don't prosper without time and attention, they'll try to find ways to support those relationships—at least within the bounds of what's possible for them.

But SP Threes are probably never going to be the sort of people who like to just hang out without any sort of agenda (or who would leave their house without their Blackberry or iPhone). Instead of relaxing them, this lack of structure would probably make them nervous (it's as if having a lot of unstructured time tends to make them lose their grip on who they are). What helps SP Threes is giving them a concrete procedure they can follow to avoid over-managing their lives. They need that kind of structure if they're to learn how to let go of the need to be constantly involved in security-ensuring activities.

SP Four—The Artisan. *Independent, persevering, sensitive, vulnerable, outspoken, artistic.* The SP Four is a strange combination of great sensitivity combined with great determination and fierce independence. The motto "never let them see you sweat" must have been invented for the SP Four. Unlike other Four subtypes (especially the SX Four), they tend to keep their emotions tightly under wraps—they can feel a certain pride in not letting others know how vulnerable they really feel. But the main purpose is defensive; the vulnerability is so great (much like an SP Eight) that an SP Four just doesn't feel comfortable revealing her sensitivities to the outside world. So she has to learn how to avoid papering over painful emotions, especially in front of other people.

Like all Fours, SP Fours are sensitive to their physical environment and find it difficult to tolerate any environment that seems fake, ugly, or (to use a good Fourish term) "soul-destroying." So SP Fours can get very involved in creating a home environment that feeds their need for beauty, however they view it. Typically, it involves rich textures and colors, lots of textiles, pottery, tile work, and other folksy touches. These are often things that the Four has created herself. She has a particular talent for bringing together a lot of eclectic elements in a way that creates a warm, vibrant space that other people appreciate.

If an SP Four travels, she likes to take her home with her—or as much of it as she can. While this is always a tendency of people with the self-preservation leanings, it's especially strong in the SP Four. The right environment matters so much that they can be like modern gypsies (and they often dress that way, too).

SP Fours have typically been dubbed dauntless or reckless. And there is some truth in the idea that they have an unusual ethos regarding safety and security. All SP subtypes tend to ensure their safety by certain predictable means (saving money, seeking shelter, protecting the family, etc.), and so do SP Fours. At the same time, SP Fours often see security in a different light. While they value (and can even over-value) personal comfort, they have in them the same yearning as other Fours to find out who they really are—to get to the bottom of themselves, because they sense that this is the only really lasting way to achieve a sense of security. So when an opportunity to do so presents itself, the SP Four will often seize upon it, even if it means engaging in behavior that looks (and sometimes is) perilous in some way. It's a high-risk strategy that may or may not work. But the intent is not to self-destruct but to effect some kind of radical shift in their situation.

Most of the time, however, the SP Four is doing ordinary stuff, just like everybody else. Despite their outer stoicism, SP Fours are often lonely people who really appreciate a friend. Although their independent streak and outspokenness can put people off, they often have interesting things to say. For someone willing to put up with their quirks (or even appreciate them), they can make loyal and trustworthy friends.

SP Five—The Archivist. *Self-insulating, sensitive, curious, circumspect, information-seeking, archive-keeping.* SP Fives are the ultimate self-preservation types. Often called "Castle" Fives (because they consider their home—or at least their room—their castle), they're the most self-insulating subtype around. I call them Archivists because they have an amazing ability to retain stuff of all kinds, both intellectual and physical. I thought about calling SP Five "The Keeper of the Scrolls," in deference to the idea that they give the impression of needing to retain everything for some greater historical or esoteric purpose than most people can easily grasp. If we don't take this impulse into account, we're apt to judge their desire for "stuff" too harshly.

On the other hand, SP Fives often need help getting rid of stuff—at least the physical kind—although they seldom welcome it. They may be quiet but it doesn't mean they are pushovers. When you suggest that they throw some of their stuff out, they may say nothing, but it would be a mistake to assume they're planning to comply. More likely, they're simply hoping you'll eventually forget the request.

Not all SP Fives accumulate actual physical stuff—some of them just accumulate knowledge. But the tendency to hoard is definitely there, one way or another. The SP Five can be like an accumulator and doesn't know how to stop accumulating (something like the SP Three who doesn't know when to stop working). The problem is that the SP Five tends to do so much accumulating that he doesn't know how to use everything he's collected, even his ideas. That's why it can be hard for him to write, because writing involves a lot of sorting and sifting.

If an SP Five *does* write a book or article, it's not usually the kind of thing you'd find on somebody's coffee table or in the dentist's waiting room. It's more likely to be a scholarly report or scientific tome. An SP Five's writings can be extremely condensed, even impenetrable, because he's so retentive yet detail-oriented.

Alternatively, he can experience writer's block. One of my SP friends had a terrible time with writer's block all the way through college (including graduate school). In order to write anything, he had to work out all his ideas before setting pen to paper, something he couldn't do under time pressure. Also, he could only write a paper when he genuinely had something to say. As a result, he racked up quite a few "Incompletes" during his time in school. It's not that he didn't want to write the papers; it's just that he wasn't able to write under those conditions. He couldn't unbend enough to allow his ideas to flow freely onto the page.

On the plus side, SP Fives tend to be extraordinarily caring, patient, and tolerant. Behind the castle wall is someone well worth getting to know, even if it's hard for him to show his concern in ways that are easy for most people to comprehend. Small children are particularly drawn to this Five subtype because of his gentleness and patience. And he in turn often finds it easier to relate to children than to adults, because their demands don't involve the kind of social complications that give him a headache.

Those of us who love the SP Fives in our lives can't make them less sensitive, but we can respect their sensitivities and let them know that we aren't attacking them when we try to get through their castle walls. We befriend them by respecting their need for privacy while at the same time letting them know we care for them and want to be part of their lives. We also need to step back sometimes (instead of always being the more "social" person in the relationship), so that the Five can step forward.

SP Six—The Family Preserver. *Warm but tentative, kind but cautious, protective of loved ones, traditional, conserving, preserving.* All SP subtypes tend to focus on the self and family, but it's the SP Six who's the ultimate family person. She's the one who finds great solace in family and tends to see family values as sacred. She is often a great traditionalist who celebrates cultural holidays, values lessons learned over time, and dedicates herself to preserving time-tested values. But it's the ongoing focus on the family that particularly distinguishes the SP Six from other SP subtypes.

In some ways, SP Sixes resemble SP Ones, in that both subtypes tend to be reserved and traditional in focus, but Ones are not so conservative in the energetic sense, because the energy at One is fiery; this gives Ones the tendency to be more pioneering and enterprising. Also, SP Ones tend to be more austere, even ascetic; they like their own company and don't necessarily seek out the company of others. For Ones, "the principle is the thing"; the family unit matters because it promotes healthy values. For SP Sixes, the opposite is true: the family itself as "the thing"; family values matter because they help sustain the family. Sixes sense that it's the family which forms the cornerstone for civilized society. Without it, civilization would break down and anarchy would reign. And anarchy is definitely not the SP Six's cup of tea.

Unlike Ones, SP Sixes have no particular inclination towards asceticism or going it alone—they may be independent, but they're seldom solitary. They like being part of a group, particularly an intimate group like the family. They often see the family group as foundational to their peace of mind: once it's in place, they feel freer to venture forth into the larger world.

As with all Sixes, there's a sense of apprehension that underlies their efforts—they seem more than others to be attuned to things unseen that might threaten their safety or that of those they love. So it's natural that their efforts focus on creating a safe and welcoming home environment. However, their apprehension can make them over-cautious, and caution can escalate to fear very easily, because they're mental types. So it's easy for fearful ideas to get out of hand. Interestingly, they actually seem to do quite well when real-life emergencies actually arise; it's just the *idea* of fear that scares them!

SP Sixes have a hard time feeling really calm—there's a sense of underlying agitation that tends to makes them feel uncertain much of the time. So some of the focus on tradition represents an effort to ground themselves in something substantial so they don't have to feel afraid. Their tendency to defer to authority is based on the same need for grounding: the energy emanating from a confident authority figure can help calm their energy and quell their fears. The idea of having rules to follow may also help them achieve a sense of inner poise.

Despite their fears, SP Sixes are usually kind and caring people who selflessly serve their families and communities. They often need a little support and encouragement to take the initiative. But when they do find their voice, they provide a particularly inspiring example to others who are hesitant to speak out.

SP Seven—The Bon Vivant. *Sense-enhancing, celebratory, friend-gathering, networking, fun-seeking, egalitarian.* Like SP Sixes, SP Sevens like to gather family around them—only instead of defining family in the traditional way, Sevens seek out innovative, unusual family structures (or create them from scratch). Their model of the family is usually based on an alternative, egalitarian-style support system that is more like an intentional community, collective, or cooperative than a traditional family. Even if the family starts out traditional (as a nuclear family with two parents and some kids), it tends to evolve into something that includes more people, many of whom aren't blood relatives.

For SP Sevens, family life also needs plenty of opportunities for fun and entertainment. To feel good about life, they need to create a celebratory family atmosphere. If they have kids, they often prefer to act more like friends than parents. Or to at least give their kids a big role in family decision-making.

SP Sevens like to gather to themselves every good thing in life: good friends, good food, a nice home with good aesthetics. They like to feel rich and well-supported. This "gathering of goodness" gives them a feeling of happiness and satisfaction—at least temporarily. They aren't quite as restless as other Seven subtypes but still need to give themselves plenty of options when settling down to buy a home or raise a family. If things start getting too settled, the SP Seven may start to introduce innovations or create extra fun even when it's counterproductive (for example, varying their child's routine to avoid boredom or trying out family structures that are really "beyond the pale"). Alternatively, they can become overly fascinated with food, home decor, fashion, or shopping for new things.

It can be helpful to remind an SP Seven that the Good Life isn't just about creating constant stimulation and innovation—it's about finding new ways to enjoy what he already has. The idea that people need a constant inflow of new things, experiences, ideas, etc., in order to feel alive is just that—an idea. If the SP Seven can grasp this, he can begin to get a handle on his ever-arising desires.

The alternative to novelty-seeking is learning how to enjoy life's simpler pleasures and realizing that change is with us all the time; we don't have to create it artificially. Making this shift in perspective allows the Seven to stop innovating simply for the sake of innovation. He can use his creativity to re-define the Good Life to be the life he already has—as seen from a more imaginative perspective.

SP Eight—The Weight Lifter. *Staunch, grounded, direct, honest, no-nonsense, resource-generating.* The label of Weight Lifter conjures up the image of Atlas holding up the world. And indeed this subtype has an exceptional ability to "stand and hold" whatever needs upholding. It represents an archetypal image of the person who stands alone, supporting the world by gathering and concentrating her strength. This subtype is often called the Survivor or Survivalist, and it's easy to see why—SP Eights are the folks that tend to gather about them every kind of physical resource, especially those necessary to support themselves and their loved ones in times of want. They tend to take the idea of self-preservation literally, as the preservation of the physical body. This is because, for an Eight, the body *is* the self.

This is not necessarily true of all the self-preservation subtypes. For example, SP Fours see survival as meaning the survival of the deepest or soul part of themselves and SP Sevens see it as meaning the survival of their personal freedom. But for the Eight, self-preservation means exactly what we'd expect: the maintenance and optimization of the physical vehicle. Of course, because Eights naturally see themselves as the standard by which everything around them is measured, they tend to project this body-self to include all the significant people in their lives—it can include not only the immediate family but a much larger group, depending upon their circumstances; the image of the patriarch or godfather captures the nature of this projection. It also captures the way that SP Eights establish perimeters to protect the group they define as theirs.

There's a good reason for this perimeter-setting activity. It's that despite their physical strength, the SP Eight is extremely vulnerable from an emotional standpoint. She has such a tender, vulnerable heart that she's at a virtual loss as to how to protect it. The physical defenses she erects are actually symbolic of (and often a substitute for) emotional defenses that are much harder to maintain.

The challenge for SP Eights is to allow themselves to lay down the burden of being strong all the time—and also to admit (at least to themselves) that they're not quite as strong as they seem. Those of us who care about them can give them support by becoming more grounded and resolute, so that they don't feel they have to carry the load for us all the time. We also help them by behaving in ways that show we understand the meaning of honor (no lying, no cheating, no backing out when we make a promise). Eights take such things very seriously, especially SP Eights. Once they're sure they're around people they can trust, Eights can sometimes begin to let go of the reins a little—and show us the gentle giant beneath the gruff exterior.

SP Nine—The Comfort Seeker. *Ordinary, childlike, patient, simplifying, absorbing, slow-moving.* The SP Nine is someone who's content with the simple pleasures of an ordinary life. Many people might not like to be characterized in this way, but this individual doesn't usually mind, because he's pretty unassuming and agreeable. He likes his little pleasures and routines, and enjoys the natural rhythms and patterns of the day. He doesn't mind puttering around in his house or taking care of the yard; these ordinary activities aren't boring to him, they're comforting. They allow him to be part of the flow of life, a feeling he appreciates.

Perhaps the SP Nine doesn't mind the ordinary because he senses that in reality, there's actually no such thing as the ordinary—that everything in life is special and extraordinary. And that's why he doesn't need to make his life (or himself) shiny and sparkly to be satisfied. He's capable of being satisfied with things as they are.

Most SP Nines are not aware of this attitude in a conscious way. They assume that everybody sees things the way they do, because it's just so natural for them. At the same time, this natural ability to go with the flow has its drawbacks. For one thing, it can lull them to sleep—it's just so pleasant to go along, being part of life, never making waves. It's comforting to know that we're all connected, all part of nature—that everything is just as it should be.

The Nine tendency to drift along without thinking too much is what makes Type 9 the classic "forgetting" type of the enneagram. And SP Nines tend to be even more forgetful than any of the other Nine subtypes. It's not because they're lazy, unmotivated, or unevolved, it's because they're in an emergent state—a state that represents the first step in differentiating the self from All That Is.

For the SP Nine, this self is first of all a *bodily* self, which is probably why SP Nines are so attracted to creature comforts, to the satisfactions of the physical body. It's as if they are not fully aware of the body as an entity in its own right. So when they eat, they aren't really aware of how much they're consuming. They simply eat as long as it feels good.

I've always suspected that a lot of the people we see in clinics for the morbidly obese are SP Nines who don't know when to stop eating. If the food is available and tastes good, they eat. The only way they can stop eating is to get a really clear signal from the body that will make them stop, which is why radical weight-loss surgery may help them when all other methods have failed. It works because it gives them a much stronger cue that they're full.

The vibratory rate of the SP Nine energy field also tends to be pretty slow, which is another reason it's relatively easy for them to gain weight or get out of shape. But it's also the reason that they can serve as such a stabilizing or grounding force for all nine types. Just being around an SP Nine tends to make people feel calmer and less agitated.

So SP Nines are pretty agreeable people to have around, but they can have difficulty getting motivated and really taking control of their lives. They appreciate the support of friends when grappling with big decisions and seldom mind a friendly nudge from people who care about them. At times, it can take more than just a nudge to get them moving, especially when the Nine is trying to work out personal problems, because SP Nines can experience the kind of trauma that would completely break anybody else and (seemingly) just shrug it off. The problem is that they don't really shrug it off, they bury it and then "forget" it. But the pile of buried hurt doesn't really go away. It creates a hidden cache of anger and resentment that they control by placing all their attention on outer life.

We can help our SP Nine friends by trying to draw them out, to listen to their stories, and to show our reaction when we hear something we don't like. Seeing our indignation, concern, or sorrow helps Nines to realize two things: first, that they have a right to feel upset when people abuse them; second, that they have people in their lives who truly care about them. Such insights help Nines to get in touch with buried pain, so they can heal. With healing, it becomes easier for them to consciously value their individual gifts and abilities.

Sexual Subtypes

The sexual subtype is also called "one-to-one" subtype. But the sexual subtype isn't just about sex—it's actually about the forces of creation and our relationship with them. The term "sexual" actually describes this better than "one-to-one" because it's more dynamic and elemental.

SX One—The Crusader. *Impassioned, earnest, righteous, argumentative, evangelizing, inspiring.* The SX One is something of a paradox. Here we have a nature that is intensely passionate but also highly self-restrictive. So the energy of the subtype is like the liquid contained within a pressure cooker. It's what gives an SX One his distinctly steamy disposition.

Of all the 27 subtypes, the SX One is the individual that's most likely to feel as though he's going to explode. Not just every so often, but on a regular basis. He's all too aware of this problem and will go to great lengths to combat this tendency, seeking to channel this explosive energy into some worthwhile cause.

This is why I call this subtype the Crusader; it has also been called the Evangelist. Both labels capture the SX Ones' passion to convert others to their point of view—a point of view that tends to be informed by idealistic or religious values.

SX Ones yearn for oneness in a conflicted world, so they're instinctively drawn to some greater cause or higher authority that can be the final arbiter of conflict. That is why I see the emblem of this subtype as being an individual with his hand raised toward Heaven, index finger pointed up, in a gesture of unity. It's as if he's trying to reach beyond duality by invoking a higher power.

It's ironic that although Ones are known for black-and-white (dichotomous) thinking, they have an impassioned desire to resolve "twoness" into "oneness"—to find some way to bring the two halves of the circle together. And it's in this One subtype that we see this desire most ardently expressed.

This passion for oneness is often expressed in the desire for a partner that is not really of this world, which is why we've historically seen many SX Ones find their vocations as priests and nuns. It's easier for such idealistic individuals to devote themselves to a spiritual partner or ideal than to a real life partner with distressingly human habits.

This idealism can interfere with relationships, because relationships are by nature untidy and disappointing, at least in terms of affirming a person's idealized notions of how people ought to behave. So if SX Ones aren't careful, their high-minded idealism can actually destroy the very intimacy for which they yearn, because it reinforces their tendency to focus too much on what is wrong and not enough on what is right.

sexual arena

creativity, sexuality, sensuality, dreams, visions, mysticism, union, spiritual awakening, artistic inspiration, shared values, competition, aspiration, inspiration, originality, imagination, myths & legends, dreams, drama, kundalini, sin & redemption, taboos, initiation rituals & rites of passage, alchemy, magic, heaven & hell, the underworld

This tendency to hone in on imperfection is what makes it particularly hard for SX Ones to find a steady partner. They are probably the most sharply critical of the three One subtypes; the tendency to criticize tends to be particularly pronounced in Ones with a Two wing. Such individuals place such a high premium on principle that it's hard for them to develop the kind of accepting attitude which people find attractive in a mate. SX Ones have a funny (but unfortunately annoying) habit of showing how much they care about their beloved by correcting their partner's behavior instead of loving the person for who she already is. The One thinks he's doing his partner a favor by making her into a better person; the mate almost invariably resists being reformed. The conflict is usually resolvable only if the One realizes the futility of his efforts and is able to turn his attention to reforming something other than his partner.

When SX Ones finally do find a partner, they tend to jealously guard the relationship. Why? Because it was so hard to find this partner in the first place! It's not easy to find a partner with the love, patience, and humor necessary to maintain a steady relationship with someone so full of reforming zeal. When the partner tries to break away (perhaps just to get a little breathing space), Ones tend to panic, afraid that their partner doesn't love them anymore. They may get very angry, mainly out of fear of loss. Later, they often feel acutely remorseful, falling into self-blame or despondency. It's poignant to realize that Ones are acutely aware of these tendencies, but find it hard to make them go away.

Despite their tempestuous nature and interpersonal difficulties, it must be said that SX Ones are willing to work hard on their relationships, even when it's difficult. They don't give up easily. As a result, they sometimes find the ability to break through their own inner barriers, even against great odds.

They are also willing to make considerable sacrifices in order to translate their dreams into realities. So they have a lot to offer the world, especially as spiritual leaders and social reformers. They make inspired speakers with the ability to inspire others with their passion for what is right and fair. They have a genuinely noble disposition that can cut through the cynicism of modern life.

SX Ones often have a tremendous passion for the arts and litera-ture, as well as the artistic discernment necessary to tell the difference between genuine art and faddish imitations. Their aspirations for ar-tistic excellence enable them to gain a great deal of satisfaction from creative work. Creative projects also help them channel their passion into an area where perfectionism is definitely a virtue. Combining their artistic vision with an eye for detail, SX Ones can often produce works of great beauty and lasting value.

What they most need to do is find a way to lighten up—to let off steam—so that they don't go through life in a constant state of pain-ful tension. It's through a combination of discipline, creative expres-sion, and relaxation that the SX One can learn to channel his energy in a way that brings him real love and joy.

SX Two—The Romantic. *Giving, sacrificing, emoting, doting, roman-ticizing, idealizing.* This subtype of Two is the archetype that shows up in every romantic comedy that ever came down the pike—it's the female (or more recently, the male) who just wants to find love, and will do just about anything to make it happen. Some people call Type 4 the Roman-tic, but Fours are more dramatic than romantic. It's the Two who has stars in her eyes. She's the one who just loves to fall in love. And usually, it's the Two who also loves the pursuit, who loves the whole process of seeking, finding, and winning the mate of her choice.

In the attracting phase of developing a new relationship, Twos tend to let themselves fall into the orbit of their partner, lavishing him with lots of attention while seeming to ask for nothing in return. This is a pretty good way to attract a mate but it's also a good way to set yourself up for a very lopsided relationship in the long run. The Two secretly hopes that her partner—realizing that he's got a wonderfully devoted mate—will come to love and appreciate all this support and respond by returning the favor. At the same time, the Two realizes on some level that this is an unrealistic expectation. When it doesn't come to pass, she feels justified in leaving (and thus gaining the freedom to go through the very enjoyable "falling in love" process all over again). Alternatively, she may decide to hang on, despite the disappointment of realizing that her partner doesn't really appreciate her for herself.

If this situation continues for a long time, she may take on the self-dramatizing role of martyr as compensation for her "sacrifice."

What the SX Two has to come to grips with is her difficulty discerning the difference between seeking love for the sake of companionship versus seeking love for the sake of excitement and the "thrill of the chase." Often, the chase is more interesting to her than the actual relationship, although she can be the last one to realize this. She may need to have many disappointing experiences before she gets to the point where the chase is no longer exciting. That's when she has the chance to see what it's like to cultivate a relationship based on mutual giving and receiving.

SX Twos who are particularly devotional may be attracted to a devotional spiritual practice. SX Ones can also be devotional, but devotion for Ones tends to be more idealized and ascetic while for Twos, it is more intimate and tangible. So they're often drawn to work that involves offering others some sort of personal spiritual support. (Given the devotional nature of Christianity, it should come as no surprise that many enneagram teachers consider Jesus to have been a Two and Christianity to be a Two-inspired religion.)

As with relationships, Twos have to be careful to avoid over-committing themselves when getting involved in work that involves giving, so that they don't burn out or become martyrs for the cause. The mature SX Two discovers ways to give that are intrinsically rewarding. In this way, she becomes the kind of giver for whom the joy of giving is its own reward.

SX Three—The Superstar. *Driving, competitive, winning, excelling, aspiring, dazzling, penetrating, climbing.* If SX Ones are inspiring, SX Threes are *aspiring*—they have the drive, the vision, and the personal magnetism needed to climb from lowly beginnings to the highest pinnacle of achievement. In their penetrating gaze, we see a look of determination to succeed, to overcome whatever stands in their way. They're willing and able to work with their image in a way that can dazzle the public and gain them the acclaim they seek. So success doesn't just fall into their laps; it's usually hard-won. But the rewards are great: money, fame, power, and romance—the kind of gains that we ordinary mortals find hard to imagine.

At the same time, all that glitters is not gold—and the considerable perks that come with a successful persona don't necessarily bring a happy and contented life. It's all too easy for SX Threes to become victims of their own success—for them to become so good at hyping their own image that they become exhausted trying to live up to it. It can be particularly difficult for them to make the transition from public persona to private person. To friends and family, a fabulous image is usually less impressive than the ability to be kind, sincere, and genuinely loving.

So the very image that SX Threes so successfully cultivate tends to get in the way when they're trying to move beyond image to intimacy; their impressive persona is better for attracting groupies than potential partners. The flashy image also gets in the way of self-insight, because people who get really good at projecting images tend to get caught up in those images, even when they don't want to. So the image-generating machinery also makes it hard for Threes to get to know *themselves*.

If SX Threes are serious about either self-understanding or finding closeness with others, they have to stop identifying with the persona that has brought them success. Not surprisingly, they usually find it difficult to make this sacrifice (as any of us might). That's why it often takes some sort of dramatic (and traumatic) event to make them stop and reassess their lives—a physical collapse, a drug problem, or a relationship disaster.

Spiritually, this subtype tends to be drawn to groups in which charisma and hard work are rewarded. They tend to remain within the confines of an accepted tradition, but to excel within those confines—like the character Father Ralph in the novel *The Thorn Birds*, whose ambitions to achieve high office in the Catholic Church were made more difficult because of his genuine love for a young woman. He unfortunately managed to throw off love in favor of advancement, but his success was marred by the occasional pain (and perhaps shame) he experienced because, deep down, he knew he'd sacrificed love to ambition. But it was not until the very end of his life that he fully realized the folly of such a sacrifice.

This story exemplifies the spiritual dilemma of an SX Three. It's all too easy for him to think he's after spirituality when he's actually looking for success in the spiritual arena. Sometimes, the best path for the SX Three seems to be to pursue his desire for success (whether in the secular or spiritual arena) to the nth degree, achieve it, and then reflect on his situation. It's at this point that he's in a position to determine what this success has really brought him: real fulfillment or just a gnawing sense of emptiness. If he realizes he hasn't found what he was looking for, he can use the same drive and determination that helped him achieve outer success to search for the kind of success that can genuinely satisfy his inner longings. If he's lucky, he'll still be young enough to work through the challenges that this scenario entails.

SX Four—The Dramatist. *Intense, emotional, transforming, creative, sensitive, resonating.* SX Fours are the individuals upon whom the usual stereotype of Type 4 is based. Intensely self-dramatizing, expressive, and individualistic, they're the most outwardly emotional and volatile of the three Four subtypes. Like SX Ones (a connecting point), they can be extremely critical of others and inclined toward jealousy. They tend to be competitive and can feel hostile toward those who stand in their way.

But it's because of these very extremes of their nature that they have such depth, artistry, and sensitivity. They're challenged from an early age to find a way of working with their energy that enables them to create something worthwhile but without losing their emotional balance. Like other Fours, they're seldom drawn to 9-to-5 work, instead excelling in the arts, the theater, or some other venue in which their restless but intensely creative core energy can find appropriate expression.

An SX Four is capable of acting boldly around others, but underneath the dramatic persona is an individual who often finds it difficult to form close relationships, because she's so intense and passionate. Romantic relationships tend to be tempestuous and difficult to sustain, because the intensity she enjoys is not the kind of energy that usually makes for a long-term, committed relationship. Also, like SX Ones, SX Fours tend to idealize their partners. When the partner fails to live up to expectations (which they invariably do), the Four can feel not only intensely disappointed, but emotionally abandoned.

Spiritually, they're drawn toward the extreme ends of whatever path they pursue—for example, into the shadowlands of the deep psyche or the edgy practices of a Tantric path. They're by nature edge-walkers, and they take the same risks with their spiritual lives that they do elsewhere. If they're not spiritual, they may find themselves gravitating in the opposite direction, becoming passionate advocates of radical philosophies such as atheism, existentialism, or nihilism (because of their willingness to embrace extremes).

This inner pull towards extremes is often misunderstood as the will to self-destruct, but it's more akin to the Sufi desire for spiritual annihilation—annihilation in God. Like the SX One, the SX Four seeks the end of separation between Self and Other; but where the One seeks oneness, the Four seeks its mystical twin: nothingness. It's part of the SX Four's nature to be a "moth to the flame."

In most cultures, this kind of anarchic spirituality is frowned upon because it tends to subvert conventional values and religious authority. For this reason, SX Fours can easily find themselves on the outs with their local spiritual community, which is one way they can become the tragic lead in their own life stories. They don't know how to be who they are and still remain acceptable to others. So they often go to the opposite extreme, proclaiming "I don't care what you think—I'm going to be myself anyway!"

SX Fours appreciate friends who accept them for what they are instead of asking them to conform to some societal ideal. They are grateful to people who are willing to listen to their (often idiosyncratic) views and to put up with their emotional intensity and sensitivity. At the same time, if they want to keep those friends over time, they have be willing to meet them halfway. And this means learning to become less self-dramatizing and more tolerant, patient, and receptive.

This isn't easy. It means that the SX Four must stop making unrealistic emotional demands on others and stop justifying "diva-like" behavior when those demands aren't met. She also has to give up the sense of subtle superiority that masks her feelings of extreme vulnerability. While such changes require courage, they can help the SX Four learn how to ground her energy in a way that allows it to become a powerful catalyst for positive change, both for herself and others.

SX Five—The Wizard. *Sensitive, secretive, mysterious, deep, paradoxical, eccentric, crystallizing.* Like SX Fours, SX Fives are unconventional and shy, especially with people they don't know. They tend to be not just introverted, but secretive—even mysterious. With an SX Five, it's hard to say how much of the secrecy is created and how much simply goes with the territory. It's true that SX Fives often appear to be operating in a secretive way, compartmentalizing their lives so as to ensure that no one person has access to all sides of them. But what is not so clear is the origin of this impulse, which is itself mysterious.

SX Fives seem to have access to deep (secret?) places in the psyche, deeper than thought or feeling. They can be extraordinarily sensitive to energies in the environment or in other people, and thus even more reclusive than other Five subtypes. Like all SX subtypes, they seek intimacy with others, but the intimacy they seek is very exclusive, far removed from the flow of everyday life. There is a desire for intensity in the relationship, for intensely personal sharing. The relationship may be strange or unusual in some way, sexually or otherwise.

Not surprisingly, SX Fives are excellent candidates for any work requiring a talent for keeping secrets, such as intelligence work. They often have brilliant intellects, and this brilliance—combined with their penchant for secretiveness—makes them perfect candidates for work such as code-breaking, secret weapons development, or esoteric research. On the other hand, they often have difficulty relating to other people, especially those who do not interest them. So they have to find a way to reconcile their secretive and asocial nature with the social demands of ordinary life.

Archetypally, they fit the image of a shaman, wizard, or magician. Spiritually, they can be intensely inward and extreme practitioners of meditation, contemplation, or other austere or ascetic practices. Whatever the approach taken, it often requires a great deal of focus, concentration, and discipline, as well as the ability to comprehend esoteric texts or other obscure forms of knowledge.

It can be difficult for the SX Five living in a modern-day, consumer-oriented society to find a way to fit into such a culture (although the Internet has provided opportunities to interact with people in a way that many SX Fives find appealing). But this doesn't completely solve their problem of with interacting people in real life. Sensitive friends can help them by offering gentle encouragement while at the same time respecting their boundaries and not taking offense at the Five's inability to be open at times.

The Five can help himself by taking the initiative to figure out ways he can function in the world without becoming overwhelmed. He also needs to cultivate realistic expectations in his personal relationships with others (especially relationships with non-Fives), so that he's not disconcerted when other people lack the same sense of exclusivity that he values in his intimate life.

SX Six—The Scrapper. *Feisty, badgering, death-defying, punchy, provocative, forceful.* Sixes are especially susceptible to feelings of fear and apprehension, but each subtype deals with those feelings in a different way. The SP Six looks to the family for support and the SOC Six looks to the group. But the SX Six looks to overcome fear by taking the bull by the horns—and acting the exact opposite of how she feels!

This is why SX Sixes are often called counterphobic: because they're determined to avoid showing fear. Instead, they learn how to look revved up, feisty, and (sometimes) combative. They may take on difficult tasks, trying to overcome impossible odds. So it's not surprising that they're attracted to high-risk activities of all types, such as skydiving, mountain climbing, cave diving, heli-skiing, and car racing. Part of the attraction is the need to drain off nervous energy, but the bigger attraction is the feeling of calm that comes after surviving a dangerous encounter.

Of course, not all SX Sixes are engaged in dangerous sports, but they all feel the pull to challenge themselves in ways that develop courage and inhibit fear. It could be doing something like taking on a challenging job, applying to a Ph.D. program, or enrolling in Toastmasters to overcome a fear of public speaking. They sometimes seek to overcome social fears by cultivating an especially warm, forward-moving personality that's almost aggressively engaging. The SX Six can therefore look almost Two-ish to the casual observer, although the underlying motivation is quite different. While Twos cultivate a warm image in order to develop friendships and form closer emotional ties, Sixes cultivate such an image in order to project a larger-than-life persona that both bolsters their self-confidence and wards off potential threats from other people.

SX Sixes can be quite romantic, but along with their romanticism comes a tendency to idealize their partners. They often put partners (and other people they admire) up on a pedestal. Of course, real-life people can't survive very long up there. When they fall off, the SX Six may suddenly withdraw her support, leaving the other person feeling hurt and bewildered. So it's important for Sixes to become aware of this tendency, so they can avoid setting people up for failure.

Like Fours, Sixes of this subtype can be very involved in artistic projects. But Fourish creativity arises out of the deeply felt need to express the inner dimensions of the psyche; Sixish creativity is generally less personal and more in tune with social trends.

Spiritually, SX Sixes can be all over the map. While some take on the archetypal role of defenders of the faith or religious crusaders, they can also be attracted to paths that are respectful of psychic or mediumistic abilities. Due to their skeptical nature, Sixes can also be atheists, agnostics, or skeptics (especially scientific skeptics). Other types can also be skeptical, but SX Sixes often have a contrary streak that can lead them to pull in the opposite direction of the mainstream, perhaps to convince themselves that, yes, it's really possible to go against the grain.

The behavior of SX Sixes can also be all over the map. Although they are a fear type, they tend to compensate by acting the exact opposite of how they feel. So they often look quite bold when what they're actually feeling is anxiety. Although they may be able to put on a good front most of the time, they can be prone to sudden bouts of reactivity that appear to arise out of the blue.

What they need to do is cultivate a calm center to help them stabilize their feelings, so they are less prone to reactivity. This centeredness can also help them desist from seeking out risky activities (in order to prove themselves, over and over again); so can reassurance from friends and family.

But in the end, SX Sixes probably benefit most from finding ways to face their fears alone, perhaps through daily practices such as meditation, contemplation, prayer, or breath work. Inward reflection and calming practices can help them make peace with fear in a way that high-risk activities never can.

SX Seven—The Trickster. *Enlightening, crazy, funny, will o' the wisp, tricky, astounding, joy-giving.* Combining the whimsy of the Seven and the intensity of the Sexual subtype, SX Sevens have a super-dynamic personality that makes them one of the most humorous and entertaining of all the subtypes. Their Peter Pan quality and natural charm give them a personal appeal that's hard to beat.

SX Sevens are interested in just about everything and everybody. They seem to have three speeds: fast, faster, and fastest (especially when they're young). They're often multitalented and popular with other people. So they can look like the kind of entertaining character that everybody else wants to be—like they're living a life devoid of dullness.

But the energy of this subtype is not quite what it seems; it's actually harder to handle than it looks. SX Sevens have a lot of energy to work with, all right—so much energy that they're constantly juggling to stay on top of it. They're tricksters not so much in the sense that they are dishonest or deceitful, but in the sense that they have a tricky energy to deal with—and if they can't figure it out, it can turn on them. But as long as they keeping moving, they're safe. Or so they think.

SX Sevens seem to be every person's fantasy lover—gentle, considerate, and utterly fascinated by their partner. Like SX Ones and Sixes, they're prone to idealize their partners, but at the same time, they can find the prospect of settling down unnerving. So they dance into our lives, charm and delight us, and then dance their way out the door.

Although they're highly imaginative and creative, often what they create is actually "fantasyware," because it's hard for them to stay put long enough to turn it into anything else. The same difficulty crops up in their spiritual lives: they easily touch Heaven but have a hard time staying there (because they get bored with spiritual practices).

So the one that most often gets tricked is the Trickster himself: thinking himself above the fray, he gets caught up in the illusion that he'll always be able to make life whatever he wants it to be. His challenge is to come to terms with life as it is, not as he imagines it to be. In the process, he'll probably run into a few demons or skeletons in the closet that he managed to sidestep in the past. Coming face to

face with his fears (without dancing away) is what he has to do if he
really wants to gain a handle on his energy (instead of falling into the
role of Sorcerer's Apprentice). People who care about the SX Seven
can support him by making it clear that they enjoy his company even
when he's feeling quiet or sad. This encourages him to slow down
and catch up with himself, so he has a chance to pull something new
out of his bag of tricks: himself.

SX Eight—The Knight. *Powerful, charismatic, chivalric, noblesse
oblige, grave, committed.* SX Eights are like characters from the Age of
Chivalry—brave, bold, and full of desire to quest for the Holy Grail.
They tend to be larger-than-life characters who believe in the values of a bygone era, values such as honor, courage, integrity, and
justice. They expect others to live by such values, too (because they
are obviously the "best" values). When people don't share this view,
SX Eights can take this as a personal betrayal—and feel justified in
seeking retribution.

SX Eights are extraordinarily intense and need outlets for that
intensity—usually physical outlets, since they're gut types. They're
well aware of the power of their energy and take it seriously, because
they see what can happen when it gets out of control. Of course,
when they succeed in channeling their vitality into some constructive
activity, they can accomplish amazing things.

Mentally, SX Eights live in a heroic world, full of larger-than-
life images and archetypes. Sexually, they seek intense, over-the-top
experiences that take them right to the edge. They like to take on a
dominant role and often seek their opposite: someone willing to take
on a submissive role. So temperamentally, they're the polar opposite
of SX Fours (the "moths to the flame"). On a deeper level, though,
SX Eights actually long for submission—to find a partner to whom
they can completely surrender.

The extremes that they seek can be difficult to find, so SX Eights
are more often disappointed than fulfilled. The result can be feelings
of intense frustration and anger. If they take these feelings into a
relationship, they can become overly dominant, even domineering.
It's as though they can't help but push the limits. If their partner

doesn't know how to push back, he'll either get steam-rolled or swallowed up.

SX Eights can benefit from realizing that their personal code of conduct is not necessarily the best standard by which to judge everybody else—that there is more than one valid set of personal values in the world. They can also benefit from finding practical ways to develop self-control, so their big energy stays under wraps until it's needed. It's important for Eights to take the initiative to do this for themselves, because they're usually not very good at adhering to standards developed by others. So ultimately Eights usually have to set their own limits and develop the habits necessary to make them stick.

At the same time, SX Eights can be transformed by intensely intimate relationships that enable them to relinquish control and become completely receptive, even for brief periods of time. Such experiences help them get in touch with buried anger and pain, so they feel emotionally alive and relieved of inner tension which could otherwise build to dangerous levels. While it's a cliché these days to speak of "finding our inner child," for SX Eights, this can put them in touch with parts of themselves that need healing.

SX Nine—The Mystic. *Serving, receiving, loving, being, refreshing, soothing, accepting.* Being in the presence of an SX Nine is like stepping into a warm, soothing pool of water. Unlike most sexual subtypes, SX Nines are not overtly intense. At the same time, they tend to be very appealing, although in a quiet (and perhaps mysterious) way.

In some way, when we're with a SX Nine, it's almost as if he's not actually present. He can seem to take up no space at all, at least not in the personal sense. At the same time, in his presence, we often feel a sense of healing, release, or love. It's not because he's intentionally doing anything; it's more like he's in a state of *being* that has healing qualities. Around the SX Nine, we're reminded of the things that make life worth living: magic, nature, childhood, and home.

SX Nines are so immersed in their environment that they usually have a hard time seeing themselves as separate from it. They're very attuned to nature, and they get great sustenance from activities involving nature—hiking, weeding, or simply sitting in their garden.

They know how to appreciate the ordinary, everyday parts of the natural world: the plants, the small animals, or the pebbles on the beach. As a result, they have a way of transforming the ordinary into the extraordinary. When we're around them, we tend to have the same experience, which is one reason they so easily touch our hearts. As partners, they're gentle, devoted, and caring. So they can seem rather like Twos, but are more unassuming and less effusive. Their caring is quieter and often takes the form of acceptance and tolerance for difficult behavior. Their healing presence can "soothe the savage beast," so they often attract partners who have been wounded by life in some way.

Like SX Sevens, SX Nines are wonderfully imaginative, and they can have similar problems getting swept away by an overactive imagination. But the energy at Nine is much slower and more languid, and the fantasy is more richly ornamented and "storied."

SX Nines find it blissful to be drawn into an intimate relationship where they can lose themselves in the Other, although the desire to merge can be so compelling that it overrides common sense. It's all too easy for them to settle for a less-than-wonderful relationship, because they find it easy to notice only the good things about the situation and forget the rest. It can take a *lot* of abuse to make them realize that things have gotten out of hand.

Because many SX Nines have a healing presence, they're often found in the healing professions, especially those involving hands-on body work. They're also natural mystics (and nature mystics) who are particularly drawn to paths in which they can have some kind of direct experience of nature, essence, or God.

Ironically, SX Nines can actually be *too* spiritual, developing a problem called "spiritual bypass," where a person so prefers a "merged" state of consciousness that he never fully incarnates as an individual (and thus never realizes his full potential in life). Although most of us think of spirituality as a good thing, it can be too much of a good thing for people of this subtype. The desire for melting into something greater than the self can cause them to lack discrimination when choosing an intimate partner, simply because they're looking more for an energetic experience than for intimacy in the personal sense.

SX Nines looking for intimacy need to be encouraged to seek not only a relationship where they can merge, but one where they can *emerge*—where they can learn how to be fully present to themselves, their partner, and the relationship. Friends of the SX Nine can support this process of emergence by letting him know how much they appreciate his individual gifts and encouraging him to develop them further. The Nine who knows himself is the person who can find not just any partner, but exactly the right one.

Social Subtypes

Social subtypes see themselves less as individuals and more as participants in something bigger than themselves—a neighborhood, community, city, state, or nation. So they tend to be preoccupied with the group and things that affect the group, not the individual. Of course, the exact nature of the preoccupation varies. It could be with a certain political party, set of ideals, utopian vision, social theory, code of conduct, educational approach, philosophy of life, religion, or world view. On a less lofty level, it could be the preoccupation with pop culture, the latest trends, staying current, and anticipating what's coming next. Whatever it is, this preoccupation takes the individual out of the personal realm and catapults him into a broader social context.

social arena

neighbors, community, public areas, government, laws, courts, institutions, organizations, companies, culture, race relations, ethical systems, manners, humanitarian projects, politics, systems theory, social activism, dharma, in-group/out-group dynamics, social status, prestige, duty, games, socializing, gangs, the military, the world

SOC One—The Lawmaker. *Dignified, magisterial, lawyerly, self-assured, prescriptive, respectful.* Whenever I think of this subtype, the image of Charlton Heston in *The Ten Commandments* always pops into my head. The movie was made in the 1950s, at a time when the idea of the patriarchal figure of the Lawmaker was designed to inspire a kind of awe that has now gone out of fashion. Moses is the ultimate example of this larger-than-life social archetype: the righteous man who by his righteousness has earned the ability to proclaim the truth to the people.

Although modern SOC Ones might like to be lawgivers in the grand old tradition of Moses, nowadays (if they're lucky) they get to participate in just one part of the lawmaking process—legislating, governing, or judging (not all three!). We find many Ones involved in some way with developing or interpreting codes, laws, and standards. As enthusiastic policy makers, advice-givers, and parliamentarians, they're the obvious person to interpret obscure points involving Robert's Rules of Order or Emily Post's rules of etiquette.

Like all Ones, SOC Ones are serious, at least as compared to other people. And nowhere is this seriousness more evident than in their sincere (even earnest) desire to make the world a better place—a task obviously best accomplished by the imposition of rules, standards, or guidelines for human conduct. Because of their seriousness, SOC Ones can be an easy target for jokes. But although we may poke fun at the (sometimes straitlaced) One, we ignore his concern for law and justice at our peril.

SOC Ones remind us that life without law can be pretty awful. They make us pay attention to the importance of taking values seriously—seriously enough to incorporate them into the codes by which we live. It's all too easy in a free society to take our values for granted. It's the Ones of the world who make sure that we don't stay complacent for long: they wake us up, shake us up, and make us confront our lack of candor, whether we like it or not!

On a personal level, SOC Ones are usually not very approachable, at least not in a casual way. They tend to be formal (even distant) in demeanor. And they don't unbend very easily. Their attention is more on abstractions such as principles, rules, and values than on making new friends or having a fun time. So it can be a challenge to get them to relax and let down their hair.

Behind the formality is often a shy person who actually doesn't know how to relax, or at least finds it difficult. The problem is that SOC Ones hold such high standards for personal conduct that these standards can never actually be fulfilled by a real-life person, and so the

One almost inevitably feels that he's missed the mark, simply because he's human and makes mistakes. This can make him painfully self-conscious and socially inhibited. But he actually would like real human contact, so he's truly grateful to be drawn out of his rather stilted world of archetypes and ideals. To help the SOC One come out of his shell, it's helpful to respect his reticence and yet be persistent in seeking out the very real human being that is waiting to be discovered.

SOC Two—The Diplomat. *Interested, congenial, positive, engaging, attentive, conversational.* If SOC Ones are interested in social issues from an idealized, abstract perspective, SOC Twos are interested in such issues from a deeply personal, emotional perspective. So they're likely to get involved in humanitarian causes which allow them to be personally involved with those they help. This is why they're often supporters of causes involving child and animal welfare, work that serves the disadvantaged, or any other work that gives them the chance to feel that they're making a personal contribution. This tendency is especially strong if they have a One wing (think Mother Teresa). In bygone eras, SOC Twos were the ones who did missionary and charity work. Because they like to work directly with people, they tend to be more "hands-on" and personally involved in humanitarian work than SOC Ones.

SOC Twos are also among the most sociable of the subtypes. They're always thinking of ways to help people connect with one another. They enjoy the challenge of seeing how well they can match up the people they know, either romantically or just as friends. (The time-honored figure of the matchmaker was probably a SOC Two.)

It's no surprise that they like to take charge and create parties and other social events—the kind with panache. (This is especially true if they lean toward Three.) They're drawn to professions where they can serve groups in a personal and special way (for example, catering, baking, teaching, ministering, counseling, or coaching).

SOC Twos are natural diplomats who know how to skillfully navigate their way through a variety of social situations. They know just what to say and how to say it, instinctively understanding how to make people feel at ease. They seek recognition for their efforts, but often prefer one-to-one expressions of thanks (rather than a public announcement) because it's more personal and meaningful to them.

The challenge for SOC Twos is learning how to play the role of social facilitator in a way that enables them to make good use of their skills but without getting overly involved in people's lives or overcommitted to social causes. They must learn how to say "no" to unreasonable requests for help and to set realistic goals when stepping into demanding social roles, so they don't always have to become heros to get the job done. The catch here is that they also have to surrender their desire to cultivate an image of heroic self-sacrifice, and this is not so easy for an individual seeking to see her self-worth confirmed by the approval of others. The Two who does not know how to come to terms with this issue will eventually find herself burned out and disillusioned.

It may be helpful for SOC Twos to realize that once they transcend the need to be social heros, they become much more effective at doing what they do best: bringing magic into the realm of public life. Letting go of the desire to seek personal recognition allows them to concentrate on creating truly memorable social events—the kind that change people's lives. SOC Twos who know how to create this kind of magic don't need personal recognition to know their efforts are worthwhile: they see it every time they look at the joyful faces of those who are inspired by their efforts.

SOC Three—The Politician. *Leader-like, politic, polite, image-conscious, team-playing, cooperative.* SOC Threes were born to excel in large organizations or other public arenas. Like SOC Twos, they're skilled at navigating in a group but their focus is less on interpersonal relationships and more on achievement in the context of a team effort or other group activity.

SOC Threes like to see their group excel. But they also like to be "first among equals"—to distinguish themselves as high-achieving individuals within the group. Unlike Twos, they don't put their own needs last and the group's needs first; they see both as important. So SOC Threes are instead champions of the "win-win" philosophy of group dynamics—the one that says to people, "I'm a winner and you can be one, too."

This approach is what makes them adept politicians. They really believe what they're saying, which is why they're so good at convincing other people to adopt their ideas. SOC Threes aren't just politicians in the political sense, but in the sense of being someone who is "politic"—who's a master of group dynamics. Because they're not inhibited by the need to hold themselves back (while promoting others), they exude a lot of confidence, and this makes people want to follow them. They also know how to give energy to others without losing energy in the process, and this makes them effective leaders.

SOC Threes know not just how to lead but how to delegate. They know how to make skillful use of other people's talents. They especially excel at large-scale event planning and organizational management. Watch any TV show on elaborate weddings and you're likely to see a SOC Three in charge of the event.

I recently saw a program about a beautiful facility that could be rented out for very plush weddings. Because it was so popular, the weddings were tightly scheduled; any deviation in the schedule would be disastrous. The person in charge was an obvious SOC Three—an impeccably well-dressed, supportive woman with nerves of steel. She knew exactly how to make sure things ran according to schedule by mobilizing her able staff and not allowing herself to become rattled by small problems.

However, the same nerves of steel that enable a SOC Three to mobilize a group under stressful conditions become a disadvantage in intimate relationships, where sensitivity matters more than the ability to mobilize a team. So it's not surprising to hear that intimacy can be tough for SOC Threes. They have a double whammy in that department, because they have both the Three-ish inclination toward emotional insensitivity and the social subtype's natural inclination to relate to groups, not individuals. Thus, they naturally view people as potential clients or team members; it's hard to step out of this role just because they're not at work.

The trick for SOC Threes is to really understand that working with people in organizations is very different from working with people as individuals. They have to learn what it means to have relationships that are truly personal (not just professional). This means to be not just cooperative but *vulnerable*, not just friendly but *emotionally responsive*. Most of all, they need to cultivate the ability to notice those moments when they find themselves striving to manage those closest to them instead of simply loving them.

SOC Four—The Social Critic. *Aristocratic, reserved, refined, artistic, critical, self-conscious, shy.* Like SOC Threes, SOC Fours are well-aware of group dynamics, especially in-group/out-group dynamics. But unlike SOC Threes, they find it difficult to overlook the emotional dimensions of group politics. They see beneath the surface of things, and are especially sensitive to the emotional nuances of any social interaction. This emotional sensitivity can be socially inhibiting. Although they would like to have friends, they're all too aware of the fact that many relationships look better than they really are. Scratch the surface, and you find something quite different than what is projected to the outside world.

SOC Fours are also sensitive to the emotional currents within larger groups, especially when those currents are violent or destructive. Where SOC Twos see themselves as serving the group and SOC Threes see themselves as organizing the group, SOC Fours see themselves as *reading* the group—and often, they don't like what they read. They find it disturbing and scary, much like a SOC Six. But where the Six will try to contain her fears by bolstering the group, a Four does the opposite. She either withdraws or confronts, so she can avoid being inundated with the energy of "the herd."

The SOC Four is someone whose attention is on the group but who does not really see herself as part of the group. Much like a Five, she stands apart, surveying the group without feeling like she really belongs. But unlike a Five, the SOC Four can feel very critical (and vocal) about what she surveys, especially where matters of taste, artistry, or emotional authenticity are concerned. She is usually artistically discerning, which is why we see so many people of this subtype involved in fashion design, high-end photography, or other artistic endeavors. The SOC Four often makes an excellent art critic because she not only has an eye for design, but knows how to articulate her views. She can also be drawn to social causes, especially if her tie to One is strong.

Unlike SOC Fives, SOC Fours lack emotional detachment, which tends to make it emotionally stressful for them to participate in groups.

Despite their reserved manner, they can't help but care what people think of them. They may not really like the group, but they're still devastated when they feel slighted or excluded.

This conflict between the desire to belong and the desire to point out group deficiencies is not easily resolved. But it can be somewhat mitigated if the Four can learn how to *see through* the emotions of the group—to relate to the group at a more transpersonal, less emotional level. This is akin to piloting a plane caught in a storm to an altitude above the clouds; it can be done by focusing less attention on emotional undercurrents and more attention on higher goals. It's also helpful for the SOC Four to realize that (a) it's not up to her to personally save the group from itself and (b) even deeply conflicted groups can still accomplish a lot of good.

SOC Five—The Professor. *Theorizing, intellectualizing, researching, processing, educating, imparting.* The SOC Five is a professor, although not necessarily in the sense of being a member of the academic community (although this is not uncommon). He's a professor in the sense of professing (claiming) to know something. The SOC Five makes a claim—a claim that he understands the nature of something in a way that gives him the right to impart it to others.

Most Fives are interested in knowledge for its own sake, but SOC Fives are the ones most likely to want to share this knowledge with others, often as teachers, especially those with advanced knowledge. Sharing information as a teacher enables them to share their knowledge while retaining the kind of control that enables them to avoid getting socially entangled in group dynamics. Like SOC Fours, they tend to think of themselves as a little bit above the group, so teaching gives them a certain prestige that they enjoy.

SOC Fives particularly admire rationality and intellect. I was once interviewed by a SOC Five psychology professor for a research assistantship. The first thing he did was to ask me a physics question. It had nothing to do with the job; he just wanted to see if I was intelligent enough to work with him!

Despite their reservations about other people, SOC Fives are the Fives most likely to seek public recognition. They can be surprisingly opinionated about social and political issues, and they tend to be people who don't mince words when giving you their opinion. It's not that they seek out conflict, it's just that they don't necessarily care enough about social norms to make a big effort to avoid stepping on toes.

Both SOC Fours and SOC Fives tend to manifest the opposite of social behavior—they seem to socialize in a way that can look antisocial to people. It's not that they are really trying to cause problems, it's that they see the world in a different way from others. A SOC Five is especially apt to see the world in a way that seems odd or unusual. At the same time, he often has genuinely brilliant insights that have the potential to revolutionize our thinking. But the brilliant and odd are frequently mixed together, and it can be difficult for the Five (or anybody else) to separate them.

As with most Fives, SOC Fives don't always find it easy to communicate their insights because their thinking tends to be complex. So when they decide to communicate, either in speech or in writing, the thoughts often come out in a form that is unconventional and therefore hard to follow. But SOC Fives are motivated to establish contact with other people. They're also interested in gaining public recognition for their ideas, which is why we see SOC Fives well-represented among authors of scholarly journals and monographs. They also make good use of the Internet as web site originators, chat room participants, and bloggers.

SOC Fives are among the most intriguing of the 27 subtypes in that they are a study in contrasts. On one hand, they tend to be introverted and shy; on the other, they feel drawn to interact with other people, often by sharing the fruits of their intellect. So there is a somewhat poignant quality about them, in that they feel attracted to participate in community life but lack the kind of social ease that would make such participation comfortable.

However, as excellent problem-solvers, SOC Fives do nevertheless figure out ways to play a part in the community. They enjoy exchanging ideas with colleagues. They also gain satisfaction from helping students learn. Some of them even manage to achieve the kind of public recognition which ensures that their ideas will play a permanent role in shaping the thinking of future generations.

SOC Six—The Guardian. *Dutiful, protective, service-oriented, sincere, devoted, community-minded.* SOC Sixes appreciate the value of service. As a result, they are the mainstay of neighborhood, religious, and volunteer groups in every community. They enjoy not only the communion of being with like-minded others, but the feeling that their efforts are helping create a better, safer community, nation, and world.

The motto of the police, "to protect and serve" is based very much on a SOC Six model of the world. So it's not surprising that social Sixes are well-represented among police officers, fire fighters, and military personnel. While SOC Ones like to write the laws, SOC Sixes like to uphold them. Both groups see the value in law and order, but for Ones, their conviction arises out of idealistic conviction; for Sixes, the reasons are more pragmatic.

My father, a Six, used to stress the practical value of staying out of trouble. He was a classic SOC Six supporter of traditional values. But he found it hard to say why these values mattered so much, especially since he wasn't a religious man. His conviction was rooted in a Six's view of the world, a view that I as a Four found hard to understand. When I questioned him, he'd get frustrated. Why couldn't I see what was so obvious to him? It wasn't until I found the enneagram that his conviction began to make sense.

What matters about traditional values is the way they create a stable social framework. Since Sixes tend to have difficulties feeling safe in the world, anything that promotes a feeling of safety is attractive. SOC Sixes are especially aware of the potential of large groups to either create or destroy the peace, so they actively seek out the groups that they think have the ability to promote civil order.

While it may take them some time to check out the credentials of a group they might join, once they're convinced that the group is on the up-and-up, they become extremely loyal members who will do almost any task that's required for sustaining it, even unglamorous tasks avoided by others.

The challenge for SOC Sixes is to avoid over-identifying with their special group. Ones like to create the rules for defining the group; Twos and Threes see the group as the backdrop for developing the self; and Fours and Fives stand apart from the group (even the social subtypes). At Point 6, there's a sudden awareness that the group it-self is of value—so much so that "True Believerism" can become a problem.

It's helpful for a SOC Six to realize that although groups may be able to protect the community and provide social support, they're not a panacea for problems. Although group membership can make a person feel both more secure and valued, too much reliance on the group promotes conformity and erodes independence. So like SOC Twos, SOC Sixes need to learn how to enjoy participating in a group for its own sake, not just because of secondary gains.

SOC Seven—The Visionary. *Ingenious, amazing, utopian, far-seeing, idealistic, envisioning.* SOC Sevens are the social visionaries of the enneagram. They're the ones with the imagination to envision innovations in human culture, often on a sweeping scale. Sevens are known for their flashes of insight, and for SOC Sevens, these insights take the form of plans and possibilities that have the potential to create a whole new kind of human community.

In this sense, SOC Sevens resemble SOC Twos. Both are networkers, but the Two's focus is more hands-on and personal while the Seven's focus is more abstract and futuristic. Twos like to connect people while Sevens like to connect ideas. Twos are often satisfied working within the existing social structure while Sevens are drawn to revolutionize that structure in some way. Although not all Sevens might call themselves utopians, their ideas about human culture and society certainly tend to be idealistically unconventional.

SOC Sevens like to work in fields that require cutting-edge thinking, a sensitivity to collective trends, and the ability to envision future outcomes—fields like architecture, urban planning, high-tech computer networking, or fashion design. They also make excellent facilitators who can easily read the energy in a group and skillfully support a group in its efforts to arrive at consensus. They're generally well-liked in this role, because they don't try to force their personal agenda on the group but are good at eliciting participation from others. When organizing a group, they often favor some kind of flexible, egalitarian approach that allows everybody an equal say.

It's easy to admire their lack of interest in becoming an authority figure, but we have to remember that by declining power, they also avoid the responsibility that such power brings. By facilitating instead of leading, they become well-liked and influential with few strings attached.

What can be hard for SOC Sevens is to get grounded in a way that really allows them to translate their visionary ideas into practical realities. It's often easier for Sevens with an Eight wing, because the energy of Point 8 is so concrete and down-to-earth. At the same time, an Eight wing can also confer a tendency toward power-tripping and inflationary imaginings. So SOC Sevens who want to put their ideas into practice have to steer a steady course between flakiness and grandiosity. The support of friends and partners can help keep them on track, both personally and professionally.

SOC Eight—The Leader. *Guiding, leading, supporting, encouraging, enforcing, reinforcing.* Generally speaking, Eights are not the most diplomatic people in the world. By nature, they tend to be such rugged individualists that they can be like grizzly bears, alone in their personal domain (even when they live with others!). Eights experience the bigness of their own energy in such a vivid way that it can be hard for them to notice the energy of other people, much less appreciate its nuances. But the SOC Eight is more aware than other Eights of social norms and nuances—and this is why she's more tolerant and flexible in responding to the needs of a group. I call this subtype the Leader because it's the place of those who know what real leadership is all about: the ability to lead by example.

SOC Eights are the combat leaders that personally lead their troops into battle or the fire captains who are first in/last out of the burning building. SOC Sixes also perform acts of great bravery, but the motivation is different. While Sixes rush into the fray to gain mastery over fear, SOC Eights do it because they have the strength to do it (and therefore the responsibility).

The challenge for SOC Eights is learning how to cultivate leadership skills based on more than physical bravery and gut instinct. This usually means developing greater social sensitivity and better communication skills, and this is never easy for Eights (even SOC Eights).

They need to realize that effective leaders have to do more than just lead the way—they have to listen, facilitate, and empathize.

Eights who lack such skills can get into trouble as leaders, because they tend to demand more from their followers that they can give. I'm reminded of the incident where General Patton (surely an Eight) slapped a soldier across the face for what he considered a cowardly attitude. (This was a soldier who was in the hospital suffering from what we'd now call post-traumatic stress syndrome.) Even during World War II, this incident caused such a scandal that Patton was relieved of his command.

SOC Eights who "round out" their natural leadership ability by cultivating good social skills can become the kind of leaders who win not only on the battlefield, but in many arenas of life. While it's not easy for the bombastic Eight to develop diplomacy, any steps she makes in this direction are a real plus, because she gains the power not just to lead, but to develop leadership in others.

SOC Nine—The Cooperator. *Responding, accepting, being part of, harmonizing, blending, homogenizing.* Most Nines like to feel they're a part of something larger than themselves; SOC Nines are particularly attracted to people-oriented activities, especially activities that allow them to seamlessly blend into a group. So they especially enjoy pastimes like choral singing, group exercising, group hiking, or group meditation; they also enjoy traveling as part of a group. They don't so much need to talk to other people as to simply *be* with them—to be part of a larger whole.

So SOC Nines tend to be cooperative group members that fit in easily and are well-liked by other participants. If it were up to the Nine, this situation would never change; he would be able to remain in this role of Cooperator forever. But in real life, this is seldom possible. Over time, Nines tend to find themselves noticing little things about people or the group that irritate them, things they find hard to ignore. Or they may find that the group is changing in ways which demand that its members take on more individual responsibility. The Nine either has to wake up or find a new group in which he can (sub-) merge.

In a dream group I attend, there was a Nine who enjoyed telling dreams but was less interested in understanding them. After a year, he had a dream that was obviously offering him new opportunities to grow, but only if he were willing to become more self-aware. He said he didn't understand the dream. Soon after, he left the group. He had come to blend in, not to wake up. At least not right away.

Waking up isn't easy for a Nine. For a SOC Nine, it means being willing to see himself as a separate and unique individual, even when he's part of a group. It may also mean taking on a leadership role, which is another way of being separate. Nines with a big Eight wing often find it easier to accept leadership than Nines with a One wing, because they're influenced by the energy of Point 8, the most leadership-oriented place on the enneagram.

Nines with a One wing are more apt to wake up because they're becoming irritated by behaviors that disturb the homogeneity of the group. A friend of mine, a Nine with a One wing, sings in a choral group. She loves the experience but finds it hard to tolerate people who sing too loudly, don't pay attention, can't sight-read, etc. While she doesn't appreciate these irritants, they do give her the motivation to ask herself why she gets so perturbed.

The challenge for SOC Nines is to find a way to enjoy group participation without losing their individuality in the process. Ironically, being in a group often gives them opportunities to find their voice (and thus to let go of inappropriate ways of expressing anger, such as becoming passive-aggressive, irritated, or stubborn). Once they gain confidence, they begin to voice their opinions in a way that is appropriately assertive but not bossy or badgering.

Friends of the SOC Nine can encourage him to become more independent-minded by not punishing him when he starts to assert himself. This isn't easy, because we're so used to the Nine being an agreeable person who always goes along with our plans. Helping the Nine to find his voice and make his own decisions allows him to grow into an individual with the ability to be a leader in his own right.

Nines actually make excellent leaders, because like Sevens, they're good at creating a cooperative atmosphere and making people feel at ease. They just need a little confidence and the understanding that they have something unique to offer as leaders.

$-7-$

Wing Types

The wings are the types on either side of each enneagram point of view. They are its next-door neighbors.

When we know our point of view, we know our core motivation and behavioral tendencies. But the influence of our point of view is affected by other factors, including its wings.

We can be affected by either wing. But usually, one is more dominant than the other, which is why many people who know the enneagram tend to identify not only with their type, but with one of its wings. People speak of being a "Five with a Six Wing" (5w6) or a "Two with a One Wing" (2w1). Some people identify equally with both wings; they're said to be *bi-winged*.

If there are actually three "wing" possibilities per type, then there must technically be 27 wing types in all. However, for purposes of simplicity, I'm just going to assume that each of us has one dominant wing, which means I'll discuss 18 wing types in all. If you're trying to type yourself and both descriptions seem equally applicable, try combining them to create a bi-winged self-profile.

I find the wing types particularly interesting because they help people to understand the types not only in isolation, but in relationship to one another. Wing types show us not just how each type is affected by its neighbors, but how each type actually transitions to the next as we move around the enneagram circle in a clockwise direction. When we look at all the 18 transitions in sequence, we can see how all the types are linked together to form a coherent whole.

A Trip Around the Enneagram

If we start at the top of the enneagram, we find ourselves in a space of anticipatory expectation. At this point, we're just about to start a new project or cycle, but haven't quite done anything yet. We're simply being in the moment, content but alert. Slowly, something begins to stir. It's subtle, and it creates a slight but definite ripple of interest. We become the Anticipator (9w1).

Energy begins to gather and move. It starts to swirl around without much form. This is a time of excitement, but also tension; we sense the need to develop a definite and precise matrix for imposing some sort of order. We are becoming the Definer (1w9).

Imposing order on chaos is not an easy task; it requires discipline and concentration. It can also be nerve-wracking, because whatever

The Wing Types

we do at the start of a project will affect that project all the way through to completion. So it's a serious business. In order to minimize mistakes, we strive to find a way to judge whether we're really on track. So we seek to establish clear standards by which to separate truth from error. Once these standards are in place, we want to ensure they'll be taken seriously. We become the Reformer (1w2).

Our efforts to this point have been based on an idealized abstraction. In order to take the next step, we need to involve others in order to humanize our ideals and also enlist support for them. As we do this, we begin to see how those ideals translate into plans with the power to help real people, especially those in need. We become the Social Worker (2w1).

Part of the joy of helping others is knowing that we're not alone. We not only enjoy the companionship of others, we also see how other people can act as mirrors for our developing self-image. Each relationship mirrors back different aspects of ourselves, and this gives us an incentive to make more friends and contacts. We're now the Socializer (2w3).

We soon realize how having a social network helps us accomplish our goals in life. But we now have so many friends and contacts that we're having a hard time keeping them straight; we have to organize our relationships. As our social proficiency and organizational skills grow, we increasingly find ourselves in positions of organizational responsibility. We're becoming the Manager (3w2).

Managing people is something we're good at, but we find that relationships can sometimes become messy and even interfere with getting things done. As we become increasingly intrigued by our work, we also become more aware of ourselves as individuals. We seek to develop the skills that enable us to shine as a Professional (3w4).

Over time, we find that being a successful Professional, while rewarding, is not satisfying our deeper needs. Once we've achieved our goals, what next? We realize that we need more than ideals (Point 1), more than contacts (Point 2), or even more than outward success (Point 3). We need a sense of significance or meaning (Point 4). So we begin to engage in our work for its own sake, getting more and more knowledgeable as a Specialist (4w3).

Despite our special skills, we feel increasing dissatisfied with living on the surface of life. We want to delve deeper, to get to the bottom of who we actually are. We continue to hone our skills but to use them in the service of self-discovery, becoming ever more focused on ways to express our deepest selves. We are now the exquisitely skilled but highly sensitive Artiste (4w5).

Finally, as we encounter the chaotic zone at the bottom of the enneagram, things reach a breaking point, and there's a dramatic collapse of the self as we have known it. The sense of "self-as-role" disappears, replaced by a new and curiously impersonal self that is less constrained by the need for social approval. We find ourselves without the need to adhere to social norms or even to maintain social appearances. We are now the Iconoclast (image-breaker) (5w4).

However, we soon discover that it's exhausting to go around breaking other peoples' images all the time. Also, they don't seem to like it very much. So for the sake of convenience, we allow our natural curiosity to lead us in a new direction, into a space of pure thought and reflection. We find it extremely satisfying to become the Thinker (5w6).

The more we think about things, the more we realize how complex life really is. This understanding begins to make us a bit nervous. It also slows us down, giving us a tendency to hesitate before we act. Finally, it makes us feel our own aloneness and realize that we need companionship to avoid feeling alone and afraid. We seek ways to reestablish our social ties. How can we do this? Perhaps by volunteering to serve the needs of our family and community. We become the Server (6w5).

Through serving, we get used to being around people without feeling uncomfortably intimate. It's easier to relax if we can play a well-defined social role in the family or at work. Later, we begin to explore ways to step outside those roles. We're a little nervous about this but find that humor helps us relax in social situations. It makes other people laugh, too. We've become the Wit (6w7).

The more social approval we get, the more confident we become. We start actually enjoying life, so much so that we tend to brush aside anything that might ruin the party. We don't, after all, want to go back to that place where we felt awkward or apprehensive. We amp up our entertaining skills even more, becoming the life of the party—the Comedian (7w6).

Of course, even humor has its limits. If we're going to continue to grow, we'll have to find new venues for expansion. It's an exciting time. New worlds are opening up for us; we're dazzled by all the things that life has to offer. Buoyed by confidence and the sense that life is an adventure, we become increasingly innovative and entrepreneurial. We're now the Adventurer (7w8).

We travel to the four corners of the world, garnering every possible experience we can. We find that we adapt easily to whatever environment we encounter. We collect interesting experiences the way that some people collect stamps. But eventually, so many adventures takes its toll—we can't go on like this forever! We settle down enough to master "the art of the deal." We become the Power Broker (8w7).

But we haven't quite reached the pinnacle of achievement. We realize that while we've mastered the ability to accomplish a lot of different things, it's much more interesting to focus on just One Big Thing. We turn our entire will in one direction to accomplish some great work that will stand the test of time. As we place the final brick in the edifice we have built, we know we have finally arrived: we are the Powerhouse (8w9).

We are now enormously powerful and influential. We've managed to climb out of the laboratory of ideas (Point 5), to apply those ideas to serve others (Point 6), to expand our horizons (Point 7), and to bring all our experiences together to manifest something of substance (Point 8). We've accomplished all of our goals and have nothing left to do.

Ironically, in bringing forth our great accomplishment, we no longer have the freedom we had at earlier stages of our journey. We are now so massively powerful that we literally can't move without affecting everything around us. We're obliged to simply stand still, to be the symbol that inspires others to follow their dreams. We've become the Mountain (9w8).

But even the highest mountain doesn't remain a mountain forever. Mountains wear down and dissolve into dust, until eventually there's nothing left. This is the end of the journey. It comes as a relief, because no matter how great the accomplishment, once it's done, it's done. There's nothing left to do, no place left to go. We can't ascend any further—at least not for the moment. All we can do is return whence we came: the primordial Sea (Point 9).

In this timeless place we remain for a period, assimilating our experiences and recovering our sense of oneness with life. There are no borders or edges here; we bask in the primordial atmosphere of light and love. We experience a sense of Allness that seems to satisfy all our needs.

Then one day, there's a stir. Something begins to arise—something new, something that beckons us onward. We become vaguely irritated. We begin to anticipate some sort of change (9w1), and the whole cycle begins once more.

Thus concludes our tour of the wing types. It's amazing to me that the types are arranged in such a way that we can proceed all the way around the circle and arrive back where we started. The fact that each point bears a logical relationship to the points on either side speaks to the basic integrity of the enneagram system.

If we only look at the nine types without looking at the wings, it's harder to see how the types are actually related to one another in terms of a process model, where we move from Type 1 through Type 9 around the perimeter of the circle. But once we divide the types in half, it's much easier to see how one type flows into the next in a more or less seamless progression.

Each step of the journey involves some sort of challenge. So just what are these 18 different challenges? Let's find out.

Wing Descriptions

In our brief journey around the enneagram, we just looked at the wing types alone, without seeing them in relation to the core energy of each type. This can make it a little more difficult to see why, say, wing types 9w8 and 9w1 are more fundamentally alike than wing types 9w8 and 8w9. In this section, I give a more detailed description of each wing by type, in order to illustrate how the wings of each type are an outgrowth of its core energy.

ONE: The Perfecter

Ones are probably the most serious type on the enneagram. All Ones tend to be idealistic and perfection-oriented, but at 1w9, there's more detachment, introversion, and social reserve; at 1w2, there's more involvement, extroversion, and interest in community affairs.

1w9—The Definer. The 1w9 tends to be precise, minimalist, and literary in taste. He has the ability to focus for a long time on a single task and might use this ability to become, for example, a haiku-style poet, a maker of fine instruments, or a creator of tiny but perfect miniatures. Alternatively, he might be attracted to a spiritual path, especially one that is solitary, mystical, and ascetic in nature. The ascetic ideal tends to appeal to his minimalist nature. Whatever his focus, it will tend to reflect an innate preference for solitude and simplicity. The 1w9 tends to be emotionally reserved, even austere. He's quieter, less obviously irritable, and (dare I say) less self-righteous than the 1w2, at least in the overt sense. It's not necessarily that he's completely laid-back and agreeable, it's just that he's influenced by the Nine energy, which is much less proactive. So while the 1w9 is certainly capable of noticing imperfections, he's more inclined than the 1w2 to keep his ideas to himself. He also tends to bottle up his emotions and can become emotionally repressed if he's not careful. Like the 1w2, he's idealistic, but his idealism often has a dreamy, detached (that is, Nine-ish) quality that is more likely to find expression in solitary pursuits than in hard-driving political activism.

1w2—The Reformer. The 1w2 tends to be more outgoing, outspoken, and people-oriented than the 1w9. He's also more grounded, more apt to voice his opinions, and more in the grip of the One-ish tendency to get tied in knots over wanting to speak out against something he doesn't like versus the need to solidly justify his critiques. The 1w2 also tends to feel conflicted due to the need to satisfy his own inner standards of correctness without simultaneously violating the outer standards of society (for example, without being impolite or breaking other social rules). The 1w9 may notice a problem but he doesn't necessarily feel compelled to act on his observations, probably because he doesn't have such a strong tie to social institutions. The 1w2 is more solidly within the social orb. As a result, he finds it hard to curb the desire to intervene when he sees things that offend his sense of justice. As a result, he's often drawn to professions involving moral issues or standards—the law, social activism, or religious work. He's also drawn to work in organizations with clearly-defined hierarchies, because this makes his life more organized and clarifies who's in charge. He prefers to be at the top of the hierarchy and will work hard to get there, because he thinks he knows best and likes to be in charge. Because of his considerable self-control and self-discipline, he's often successful in this effort, as long as his temper and tendency to criticize don't alienate him from other people.

Two: The People Person

At Point 2, we find individuals for whom the term "human resource" becomes a literal truth. They cultivate relationships in a very proactive and organized way. But the wings determine whether they lean more toward social reform (2w1) or social interaction (2w3).

2w1—The Social Worker. The 2w1 embraces humanitarian ideals and is deeply concerned with the human condition. She tends to find a people-oriented cause she believes in and then dedicates herself to diminishing human suffering in some way. So she can be a passionate advocate for the poor and helpless. At the same time, her concern for others can become so compelling that it can easily become overwhelming, leading to emotional and physical exhaustion. Although she yearns to connect with others, her natural reticence makes her more inclined than the 2w3 to delimit, structure, or formalize her relationships in some way; it's harder for her to let down her hair and enjoy human companionship for its own sake. She's drawn to work that allows her to combine her interest in people with her passion for ameliorating the human condition (for example, teaching, counseling, social work, or public service). The 2w1 can get very involved (and even over-involved) in her work, so she has to be careful to remember that she has her own life and needs. That's the only way she can maintain the kind of energy reserve she needs to effectively do her work without burning out or becoming a martyr to the cause.

2w3—The Socializer. The 2w3 is freer, lighter, and less formal than the 2w1. She likes not just to make friends, but to "collect" social contacts. Like a 2w1, the 2w3 is helpful but tends to be less assiduously concerned with helping as a way of life. So she's less likely to get physically worn down or emotionally drained by too much giving. But she *can* go overboard in the socializing department—cooking for loved ones, planning social events, or committing herself to hours (or even days) of extra work, because she wants to make some social event particularly wonderful. She likes the challenge of creating the kinds of events that really help people connect with one another. As a hostess, she'll go the extra mile to make sure that everyone present feels welcome. Fun activities are often those that give something to others in a way that's both entertaining and personal; she might enjoy home decorating, selling homes, or catering. The 2w3 tends to be warm and outgoing, but can sometimes display such an eagerness for friendship that she puts people off, especially people who are more reserved. So she has to be careful to give people their own space, resisting the urge to hover over them. She also has to learn when to step back at social gatherings, so that others have a chance to contribute.

THREE: The Self-tester

At Point 3, there's a tremendous drive to excel. At 3w2, the focus is more on social organizing while at 3w4, it's on professional consulting or some other activity that allows an independent approach.

3w2—The Manager. The 3w2 tends to be a lot like a Two—friendly, outgoing, and enthusiastic. But he's less emotional and more businesslike—less of a listener-helper and more of a competent doer. He likes achievement for its own sake and derives great satisfaction from "pulling off" a significant social event. But the energy investment is more strategic and less personal than at 2w3, because Threes tend to enjoy the kind of socializing that's less intimate and personally entangling. Like a Two, the 3w2 is sensitive to the way his actions are viewed by others. But his sensitivity involves the ability to see himself in relationship to those around him—and to manage his image so that he can both get along with other people and also stand out as an individual. As a result, he often makes a good diplomat, politician, or event organizer. The 3w2 is especially competent as an organizer of large-scale events (such as celebrity weddings or rock concerts)—the kind that involve coordinating the actions of many different people when time is tight. Despite his liking for people, he can have a hard time sustaining intimate relationships because they take so much time and energy (time and energy he could be using to cultivate relationships that are less personal but more professionally rewarding).

3w4—The Professional. The 3w4 is more intense, more intently focused on his work, and more overtly competitive, both with himself and others. He has a more driven quality and can find it quite difficult to disengage from his work, even to the point of becoming a workaholic. He tends to draw a lot of his motivation from work, and this motivation has a personal quality to it—it's not just a job, it's a mission. He's more likely than the 3w2 to sacrifice personal relationships to the Gods of Work, and can have a hard time juggling work with personal relationships, even important relationships. The work itself tends to involve more expertise and specialization but less socializing. The 3w4 also tends to identify with his work and finds it painful to be separated from it, even to go on vacation. He can also be subject to flashes of moodiness or depression, which he finds somewhat alarming. But these moods seldom persist for long. If he's brave, he may try to explore these foreign emotions to some extent. But this can be a difficult undertaking for someone who finds strong emotions both scary and exhausting.

Four: The Deep Sea Diver

Fours are the artisans of the emotions, but at 4w3, emotional energy finds its outlet in more socially acceptable activities while at 4w5 there's a tendency for the individual to pursue her passions wherever they take her (even to the ends of the earth).

4w3—The Specialist. The 4w3 is both emotional and artistic but tends to have a sense of ambivalence about being pulled deeper into the psyche, especially if the culture is more oriented toward efficiency than authenticity. She also tends to channel her emotional energy into her work, which is usually creative, individualistic, and highly specialized yet lucrative—for example, interior design, web design, commercial art, or Feng Shui consulting. She feels fulfilled by work which expresses her individuality and yet wins the esteem of others. It's possible that she might rather not admit this, because it violates her belief that work ought to be done for its own sake, not to impress. The 4w3 can be somewhat flamboyant and outrageous, in part for fun and in part to provoke a response. She likes to test herself to see how much she's willing to go against the grain, to stand apart from the crowd. But at the same time, she's more thin-skinned than she lets on. She's usually quite aware of the difficulty of balancing her desire to succeed with her need to act authentically. So she can't help but hope that her need to assert herself as an individual won't actually turn others against her.

4w5—The Artiste. The 4w5 tends to be more self-contained, reclusive, and drawn to extremes than the 4w3. There's a tremendous intensity in her (remember, she's living in the depths). So it's her challenge to find a way to creatively channel this energy instead of being consumed by it. That's why most 4w5s are so intent on pursuing creative projects, especially those that allow them to be authentic and original. The work they do arises out of the depths of their being. Only this kind of approach can satisfy their inner muse and bring them some measure of equanimity. When properly accomplished, their work is not an escape from reality but a deeply felt response to a genuine calling. It reflects not only the Four's ability to tap into her deep emotions, but the Five's ability to think deeply about scientific and/or philosophical issues. This combination can make the 4w5 a gifted writer who knows how to communicate her ideas with great precision and finesse. Her tendency to go to extremes often shows up in her personal aesthetic (in the clothes she wears or the way she decorates her home). The 4w5 is often mystically inclined or completely devoted to some inner ideal for which she's willing to commit herself 100%; she is often drawn to minimalist or ascetic paths. She may feel like a slave to her art or be consumed by intense spiritual longing, much like the proverbial moth drawn to the flame (we see this especially in the SX 4w5).

FIVE: The Puzzle-solver

Fives are the most overtly mental of the types, but the thinking processes at 5w4 are more tinged with emotion and have a quality of quirky unpredictability while the mental processes at 5w6 are more logical and detached.

5w4—The Iconoclast. The 5w4 is quirky and hard to pin down; his Five-ish detachment is punctuated at times with bursts of emotional energy that crop up at unpredictable intervals. He also has more intensity than the 5w6 and the kind of burning curiosity that makes him pursue his projects and hobbies with a single-minded relentlessness that we see less often in the 5w6. Also, the 5w4 can have quite unusual hobbies that usually involve harnessing his restless intellect in some inventive way (for example, he might enjoy creating highly elaborate Lego railroad models, inventing complex computer games, or devising a radically new chess opening). Because he's unconventional, he can give people the impression that he's just some kind of crazy kook—at least until he manages to solve some problem that has beaten all the experts! Although he can dress or act in ways that are unexpected, he tends not to care much about the effect of his demeanor on other people. His iconoclasm (image-breaking) is more like a by-product of his innate unconventionality and enjoyment of the new and different. It's not usually a deliberate attempt to flaunt social conventions. Like the 4w5, he tends to combine thinking with passion (although for him, thinking comes first). He may find it difficult to reconcile his unusual outlook and lifestyle with the demands of conventional society.

5w6—The Thinker. Shy, detached, and analytical, the 5w6 better fits the usual Five stereotype than the 5w4. To the casual observer the 5w6 can seem dry and detached, although this demeanor is only skin-deep. The emotions are there but are hidden under a relatively featureless surface. Although the 5w6 may seem impassive, he's usually quite helpful if asked for assistance. He typically has many interests, mostly intellectual, technical, or philosophical. However, he lacks the penetrating, slightly "driven" quality of the 5w4. People who seek out the shy 5w6 will find a kind and steadfast friend who's also a reliable worker. But if we want his help, we have to ask for it; otherwise, he tends to keep his own counsel. It's easier for him to develop relationships in situations with well-defined social roles, especially if a large group is involved (for example, he might seek a partner by taking dance lessons or getting involved in some other activity where people are expected to approach one another. This takes the pressure off and allows him to come out of his shell). He especially enjoys activities in which he can excel (and thus gain acceptance by performing well). Less personally self-reflective than the 5w4, he can sometimes seem to lack any real sense of personal interiority but can become quite animated in discussions involving politics, social policy, philosophy, or technical matters in which he's well-versed.

Six: The Steward

Sixes tend to be sensate, apprehensive types but at 6w5, there's more shyness, reserve, and an interest in service and at 6w7, there's more liveliness, wit, and edginess.

6w5—The Server. The 6w5 is clearly shyer and more reserved than the 6w7. She's less likely to be counterphobic (that is, to be someone who deals with fear by "going where angels fear to tread"). And she tends toward introspection and working through mental problems in a careful and detailed way. Thus, like the 5w6, she has a natural bent for scientific and technical work, but she's more inclined to work within a traditional organization, institution, or framework. She's extremely conscientious but not naturally critical of others. This makes her a natural server with an unselfish work ethic. This is someone who will readily take on whatever tasks are assigned to her and do them with care and diligence. She may have definite opinions but tends to keep quiet about them, especially in public. At the same time, she can be attracted to social or political causes, especially those that focus on improving the lot of children, animals, or other groups that need protection or advocacy. However, her natural shyness and modesty make it all too easy for others to take her help for granted, so she needs to learn how to serve without becoming a doormat. She's at her best when encouraged by others to join in and be part of the group.

6w7—The Wit. The 6w7 is more animated and engaging than the 6w5, but she's also more visibly jumpy and distractible. She's discovered that humor trumps fear, so she finds she can quash her nervousness by noticing what's funny about a potentially nerve-wracking situation. Her razor-sharp wit allays her fears and also dispels the tension in the room around her. It also makes her a welcome addition at social gatherings. Receiving social approval gives her more confidence, so being witty becomes a self-reinforcing tendency (think Woody Allen). The 6w7 is typically less shy than the 6w5 and more willing to put herself in unstructured social situations, although this may seem like quite an adventure for her, because she still values tradition and feels comforted by familiar surroundings. So there's a certain ambivalence in her, as well as a tendency to alternate between seeking safety and tempting fate, which is not always terribly comfortable. The incentive for venturing forth into the world is fueled by the hunger for variety and the need to find strategies for dispelling anxiety. The 6w7 needs more variety in her life than the 6w5, and will seek out the kind of work and social situations that provide this variety.

SEVEN: The Improviser

All Sevens are mentally light and somewhat restless, but the energy at 7w6 is more free-floating, zany, and potentially manic and the energy at 7w8 is more grounded, goal-oriented, and realistic.

7w6—The Comedian. The 7w6 tends to be a lively character—funny, outrageous, and apt to pull something out of a hat at a moment's notice. He can be noticeably manic (think Robin Williams in his 20s), as if he has no "off" button. He's the original court jester, able to say what nobody else could get away with, because he knows how to get a laugh (instead of getting the ax). Because of his childlike nature, he can sometimes seem immature, especially during the first half of life. At the same time, he has the ability to lift group spirits with his wonderful imagination and ability to inspire. He knows how to bring people together in a non-hierarchical, community-oriented way—that is, if he can find within himself the groundedness to take on that kind of responsibility, which isn't easy for somebody so restless. This restlessness makes him apt to jump from thing to thing; it's easier to have fun than settle down to any kind of ordinary routine. So the challenge for him is to find a way to live lightly but responsibly.

7w8—The Adventurer. The 7w8 is steadier and more grounded than his 7w6 companion—he tends to have more physical stamina, too. He has the same high-flying energy and imagination but is more likely to find an outlet for it in activities that are both physically and mentally challenging: exciting sports, adventure travel, entrepreneurial ventures, or other fun but demanding activities. The 7w8 can be more direct and fiery than the 7w6 although this isn't his habitual state of mind. He tends to be more realistic and competitive but he competes not to discover *who he is* (as with the Three) but to find out *what he can do*—to test his powers and abilities. So he usually makes an excellent explorer in whatever field attracts his interest. This is because he's able not just to imagine something new but to put his plans into action. He also has the kind of personal magnetism that attracts the support of others, so he can really sell people on his ideas. At the same time, if he's insufficiently mature, he can make rash decisions that he later regrets or become insensitive to the needs of those closest to him. He needs to develop the maturity necessary to temper his enthusiasm with good judgment.

EIGHT: The Master

The energy at Eight is big and powerful. But at 8w7, the energy is relentless and driven; at 8w9, it's consolidated and all-encompassing.

8w7—The Power Broker. The 8w7 has the power-orientation of the Eight combined with the lively energy of the Seven—hence, the label of Power Broker. Typically, this is a person with tremendous will. She's enterprising and goal-oriented, and her goals are not just big but practical. She knows how to create "the biggest and the best," and has the drive necessary to make the impossible possible. The 8w7 definitely knows how to get things done. But she can find it difficult to delegate because she gets impatient with other people who lack her staying power (and this is practically everyone!).

She likes to lead by example, and will never ask anybody to do something that she's not willing or able to do herself. So she tends to promote her ideas not so much by talking about them but by demonstrating them—and by demonstrating her ability to get things done. But things had better be done right when she's in charge, because she takes no prisoners when it comes to laziness or incompetence. She has a short fuse and no compunctions about telling people off when they screw up (think Donald Trump). So 8w7 is the place where temper can become a major issue—and so can the need for self-control.

8w9—The Powerhouse. The 8w9 is calmer, steadier, and more circumspect than the 8w7. Although she's quieter and less apt to show her feelings, she's nonetheless a powerful influence. Much like a Five, she stands back and watches a lot. She's acutely aware of everything going on around her, especially the power dynamics. The 8w9 has immense self-assurance; she has "arrived" and she knows it. That may be why she's less interested in the limelight than the 8w7 and also more receptive to input from other people. She likes to silently evaluate people and their potential. (Who can be trusted and who can't? Who has potential and how can it be developed?) She's especially keen on finding the person whom she can mentor and eventually make her successor, so that everything she's established will continue after she's gone. She doesn't seek out trouble—she waits until it comes to her. Only then does she act. But once committed, she's a force to be reckoned with—once she makes up her mind, she's not likely to change it. She moves inexorably toward the goal and won't stop until she reaches it. This is her strength but it's also her weakness, because it can limit her ability to re-evaluate the situation, rethink her goals, and change course when necessary.

NINE: The Storyteller

The receptive, pacifying energy of Nine ranges from steady and unmoving at 9w8 to dreamy and anticipatory at 9w1.

9w8—The Mountain. By 9w8, the charged energy of the Powerhouse is becoming less charged and more inert: the massive Powerhouse is gradually becoming the unyielding Mountain. A mountain is immense but it does not move. On the other hand, it cannot *be* moved, either—and so the 9w8 represents the place of strength through standing. If a 9w8 doesn't want to do something, nothing on earth will make him do it. But most of the time, he's pretty peaceable and easygoing; he's tolerant of what goes on around him unless something really bugs him. It's then that we discover that he's not quite as imperturbable as he looks—that under the impassive mountain lies a volcanic chamber of lava that can erupt when the circumstances are right. But most of the time, this energy lies dormant, and people experience the energy at 9w8 as strong and steady. Its steadiness produces an aura of peaceful calm in the surrounding environment. The 9w8's steadiness is so great, however, that he finds sudden transitions unnerving. The fast pace of modern life is not really his cup of tea; it can make him feel like he's walking while the rest of the world is whizzing by. His typical reaction to things he doesn't like is a quiet but definite sense of annoyance which—if it becomes habitual—can harden into a crusty belligerence that lurks just under a seemingly placid surface. It's not noticeable to most people, because of the slightly dissociated quality that's typical of Nines, a quality that often seems to cut the tips off the highs and lows of their personality. But those close to the 9w8 are quite aware that what looks like placidity can actually be a stubborn intransigence that's hard to budge.

9w1—The Anticipator. Like the energy at 9w8, the energy at 9w1 is receptive. But it's also livelier, more variable, and more forward-looking. So the 9w1 has the sense of something to come—something in the air—that will make life more special and magical. He can reach toward it in his imagination, spinning tales in his head and wishing that the dream might someday become a reality. However, he usually finds it harder to act on those dreams than to imagine them. But he's often good at spinning them into the kind of stories, songs, and tall tales that inspire others to act. When it comes to ordinary life, however, the 9w1 finds it easier to get in the groove, especially with the aid of routines that help him stay on track. Dependable and cooperative, he's often happiest doing jobs that allow him to blend seamlessly into the fabric of his organization. This helps him stay calm and deal with the edgy feelings that sometimes disturb his peace. Although he's often a competent and well-liked organizer, the 9w1 is less likely than the 9w8 to seek out a leadership position, because this might bring him into conflict with other people. And conflict is something he really tries to avoid. The 9w1 does not like to rock the boat. He only takes a strong position on an issue when absolutely forced to. But it takes so much to push him to take such a position that once he finally arrives there, he can usually manage to stick to his guns.

What Can We Learn from the Wings?

The first thing we can learn from the wings is that people who have the same type but different wings are quite distinctive in certain ways. Although the core motivation may be the same, the way that motivation is expressed is not; there are different "energetic overtones." When I've viewed type panels that are divided by wing, it's easy to see wing-related differences for each type. Becoming aware of those differences helps us gain a deeper understanding of the types.

The second thing we can learn is how the wings determine the nature of the nine challenges we encounter as we move around the enneagram starting at Point 1 and moving clockwise to Point 9. The first wing represents our preliminary efforts at working through a problem; it draws quite a bit on the strategies of the previous point of view. The second wing represents the later stages in problem solving; it relies more on strategies drawn from the point of view toward which we're moving.

The third thing we gain is the ability to see the enneagram from a more dynamic perspective, one in which each type represents a step in a transformational journey. Dividing each type into two halves makes it easier to link them with the types on either side: when we "connect the dots," a meaningful whole emerges. We see how each point represents not only a personality type, but one of nine points in a transformational process. The next chapter explores this idea in more detail.

– 8 –

Nine Points in a Process

The enneagram most people know is the personality enneagram based on the teachings of Oscar Ichazo. These teachings were later disseminated by Claudio Naranjo and others starting in the mid-1970s. However, the enneagram was originally introduced by G. I. Gurdjieff, not as a way to describe human personality, but as an esoteric system depicting the nature of transformational processes. So from Gurdjieff's perspective, the enneagram is highly dynamic, energetic, and creative in nature.

It wasn't long after I started working with the enneagram that I became aware of the differences between these two approaches. The dynamism of the Gurdjieffian (Fourth Way) enneagram stood in stark contrast to the focus on fixation that I saw with the personality enneagram. I felt that finding a link between the two approaches could revitalize the latter, transforming the way we view both the enneagram itself and the nine types. So I started searching for a direct correspondence between the attributes of each *type* on the personality enneagram and the attributes of each *point* on the process enneagram. The idea was to understand how Type 1 corresponds to Point 1 in a transformational process, Type 2 to Point 2, etc.

Three years ago, I ran across some information on the process enneagram that made it easier to see the links between process and personality. In April 2007, I published an article in the *Enneagram Monthly* delineating a way to relate the two.* Since seeing the parallels between the two enneagrams, I can never again look at the nine

---

*"Personality vs. Process: The Missing Link,"; available at www.enneagramdimensions.net/articles.

personality types without also seeing their dynamic counterparts from the process enneagram. In this chapter, I'll explain how this approach works and why it's so helpful for working with the nine types.

What Kind of Process?

The process enneagram focuses on a living, creative, or transformative process—the kind of process in which something is changed from a simpler state into a state that is more complex, refined, and vibrant. What we transform can be anything; whether it's physical, mental, or emotional, the same principles apply. But to illustrate the way the process works, it's easiest to talk about the transformation of something fairly concrete.

Suppose we have an idea for a new kind of wheelchair—one that's hardier and more versatile than an ordinary wheelchair. At first, our idea is fuzzy and indistinct. We may initially see no way to translate it into a living reality. But if we keep thinking about it, mulling it over from lots of different angles, we may eventually reach the point where we get a clear idea about exactly the kind of wheelchair we want to create.

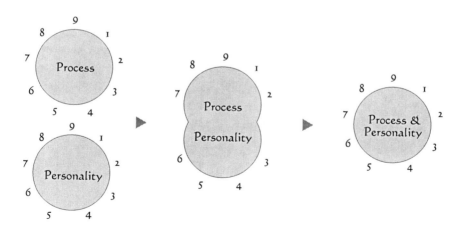

Aligning Personality with Process

Next, we have to go out and do research—talk to people, get their ideas, find out what people want in a wheelchair. We research what kinds of wheelchairs already exist, what they're made of, and whether our wheelchair design represents a significant improvement over existing models. Once we're satisfied that the idea is worth pursuing, we plan more intensively, eventually creating prototypes of our wheelchair and subjecting them to preliminary testing. At first, things go well, we feel encouraged, and we continue the project.

But sooner or later, we usually encounter problems—obstacles we hadn't anticipated. For instance, our initial prototype might be too heavy, too clumsy, or too expensive. We might run out of money or have our spouse tell us off for spending every bit of spare time on the stupid wheelchair! We might get dissatisfied, tired, afraid, or distracted. When problems like these start to pile up, we have to decide how serious we really are about continuing to pursue our dream. We have to take a hard look not only at the project, but our own motives and capabilities.

So building the wheelchair isn't just about creating a physical object; it's also about self-discovery and personal transformation. It's about testing ourselves to see whether we can truly persevere in the face of mounting obstacles.

It's during the middle phase of our project that the greatest difficulties arise, during that period when the initial excitement has worn off but the end is not yet in sight. At this point, we can't just coast along. If we're to successfully complete our project, we have to commit ourselves to it wholeheartedly and to renew that commitment every day, despite our fears and doubts. Is the design of the wheelchair sound? Can we make it affordable? Will insurance companies be willing to pay for it? We have to grapple with questions like these every day if we want to succeed.

We also have to grapple with the uncertainties involved—with not knowing where the process will take us, how it will turn out, and how it might change our lives. Only one thing is certain: if we make the decision to continue to the end, we'll never be quite the same person again. Just as we will transform our idea into a reality, we will in turn be transformed by our experience.

At a certain point, we begin to realize that we're no longer the same person who started the project. We may have started out as a dreamer with an impossible idea—but we are no longer a dreamer, but a doer (a bona fide inventor!) who will soon have a product to manufacture, market, and protect.

Facing such realities means allowing the transformational process to change us, so we can become the sort of person who can see the project through to the end. If we can make this leap—and it's a big one—we eventually find ourselves over the hump, on the downhill side of the mountain. There's an appreciable sense of elation and relief. But if we're like most people, the journey has taken a lot out of us. It would be so nice towards the end to just relax and "coast" for a while, now that things seem easier.

However, there's still more work to do, still more final touches to be added, so that our product really fulfills its potential. We have to find a way to harness our elation, so it becomes channeled toward the goal. If we manage to pull this off, we ultimately see the final result of our work: a lightweight but affordable wheelchair that's able to navigate rough terrain.

Success at last! We've finally accomplished our goal. We're able to pause for a moment and realize what we've done—to recognize our achievement and bask in our success. We're now on top of the world, master of all we survey. At least, that's how it feels.

Of course, this moment doesn't last forever. At some point, the moment of success becomes something else, something that's just part of our lives (just like previous accomplishments). If we want to make room for the next bright idea, we have to cut ourselves free of our attachment to past successes—to return to the kind of neutral, receptive space that becomes the incubator for new ideas.

Once we do, we find that we've come full circle. We've taken on a new idea and brought it to completion. Now we're returned to where we started. But it's a funny kind of "return" because it does not really represent a going *back* but a going *forward*. We not only accomplished something, but learned new things while we did it. The next project will incorporate all the lessons we've learned to this point. In this way, we and our work continue to evolve over time.

Three Stages of a Process

The process just described can be mapped onto the enneagram. And it can be done in a way that allows us to see how the nine points of the enneagram directly correspond to the nine steps of wheelchair development (or the nine steps of any other transformative project). Seeing the correspondence between the two enneagrams allows us to see the enneagram types not as *fixation* points, but as *transformation* points.

It's useful to begin by dividing the process into three main phases, each of which includes three enneagram points, starting with Point 1:

- **Beginning**—Defining goals *(Point 1)*, Humanizing goals & getting organized *(Point 2)*, Testing prototypes *(Point 3)*

- **Middle**—Grappling with deeper problems *(Point 4)*, Problem-solving *(Point 5)*, Overcoming fear & doubt *(Point 6)*

- **End**—Refocusing *(Point 7)*, Completing *(Point 8)*, Integration & incubation *(Point 9)*

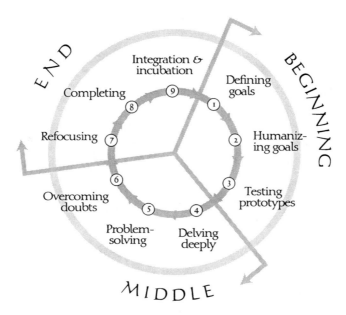

Three Phases of a Creative Process

Beginning (interest): At the start of a process, we're allowing a new idea to emerge and become more and more real in our minds. At a certain point, we start to get really serious about this idea (like the idea for a new wheelchair) and really think about what it would involve— what the obstacles would be and how to overcome them. We think through our options, determine our goals, and develop appropriate standards by which to judge our success (Point 1). We develop our initial approach with input from other people. This preparatory process helps us translate abstract goals into plans that meet real human needs (Point 2). This prepares us to develop an initial prototype, which we test and re-test, trying to get out the kinks (Point 3).

Middle (commitment): Now we encounter the problem-solving phase of the project, which can be rather like a "descent into the deep." This is the point where ideals and reality start to collide. If we want to continue, we have to come to grips with the reality that this project is going to demand more from us than casual interest. It will require emotional commitment and deep engagement in the creative process (Point 4). It will further demand all our problem-solving skills and ingenuity (Point 5). And finally, it will demand a willingness to

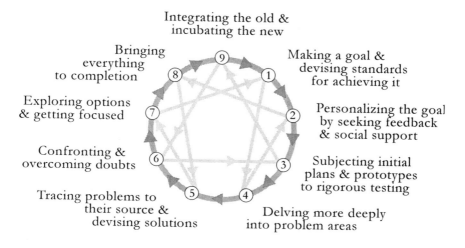

Integrating the old &
incubating the new

Bringing
everything
to completion

Making a goal &
devising standards
for achieving it

Exploring options
& getting focused

Personalizing the goal
by seeking feedback
& social support

Confronting &
overcoming doubts

Subjecting initial
plans & prototypes
to rigorous testing

Tracing problems to
their source &
devising solutions

Delving more deeply
into problem areas

Nine Points in a Creative Process

overcome remaining doubts and to make a final commitment to stay with the project, no matter what it requires of us (Point 6).

While all of these steps have their challenges, it's the final step that takes us to the transformational brink—to the point where we either totally commit or quit the project. And this is why Point 6 is such a difficult place on the enneagram: because it's the place where we confront all our remaining doubts (doubts not only about the project, but about ourselves). We know that if we go ahead, we'll be making the kind of commitment that can't be unmade. If our judgment is wrong, we can all too easily imagine the consequences. To continue, we have to face our fears and resolve them; that's the only way to move ahead.

Ironically, it's actually our fear that gives us an incentive to find resolution. But the only way to constructively harness that fear is to ground it, so it doesn't overwhelm us. A service ethic and sense of duty are helpful at this point, because they give us the kind of personal dignity we need if we are to confront fear instead of trying to duck it.

Ending (transformation): Facing our fears gives us a new lease on life—and fresh energy to complete the project. This is the moment of breakthrough. We experience a rush of relief. We find ourselves in a much freer, lighter space that's swimming in new possibilities. We're filled with inspiration and ideas. At the same time, we're too wound up to want to settle down and work (Point 7). If we manage to get a grip on our restlessness and focus our creative energy, we discover that it's possible to create a final product that is not only acceptable, but polished. We've reached our goal. This is like reaching the pinnacle of a great mountain: the view is terrific and the sense of accomplishment is gratifying (Point 8).

All the same, we haven't really reached the end of our transformational journey. We still have to take steps to ensure that our initial success is not just a flash in the pan, which means establishing the kind of structure that can stabilize our achievement (for example, establishing a viable company to manufacture our new wheelchair). We also have another less tangible but equally important challenge—the challenge of giving thanks, taking stock, and seeing how our efforts fit into the larger landscape of our lives. This may sound like a side issue, but if it's not managed well, we'll never be able to learn something new from our experience.

Then comes the biggest challenge of all: descending from the pinnacle of creation back down the mountain. This means allowing ourselves to let go of the passion that's driven us for so long, so we can come back to ordinary life (Point 9). We have to go from the "highest" place to the "lowest" (at least in terms of feeling our own power). And we have to do it in only one step.

How can this happen? It happens through *assimilation*—by taking what was outside (our accomplishment) and transforming it into something *inside*—something that becomes part of *who we are*. It might look like we're losing something as it "disappears" inside of us, but this is an illusion. Nothing actually disappears—it just changes in form. We let go, loosen up, and open up, gradually allowing ourselves to move from a position of great assertiveness to one of complete receptivity.

From the outside, this move might look like a loss—like we're losing power and gaining nothing. But it's actually a place of rest and rejuvenation. We let go of our cares and stop worrying about the past or the future. We experience the peace of letting go, of forgetting about past trials. We live in the moment, enjoying the little pleasures. Life is good.

This phase doesn't last forever, of course. (Even paradise can seem a little boring after a while.) Eventually, we begin to feel something stirring. We get a little restless; we begin to tell ourselves stories and to imagine how they might end. One day, one of these stories becomes vivid enough to really catch our interest, and we want to make it real. We begin to feel the anticipation and "what if" feeling that awakens a desire to do something new. And soon, the transformational process begins all over again....

The Nine Types as Nine Stages of Transformation

As the above example demonstrates, it's not hard to describe nine transformative steps in a way that demonstrates direct parallels between these steps and the nine types of the personality enneagram. Each transformational step can only happen when a certain kind of energy and motivation is present: *the same energy and motivation associated with the enneagram type linked to that step.* The relationship between the step and the type is not coincidental. It's *meaningful*, as we can see by looking at the chart on the next page.

How Type Relates to Transformation

Pt ▼	Type Motivation	Transformational Task
1	To perfect ideals & develop high standards for personal conduct	To perfect the standards needed to manifest an ideal
2	To meet people and create social networks	To translate ideals into plans that meet real human needs
3	To test ourselves in order to determine our abilities & improve our performance	To "reality test" our ideas in order to determine whether they're worth pursuing
4	To explore the depths so we can embrace what is most authentic about ourselves	To explore the depths of a problem & make an emotional commitment to resolve it
5	To discover the truth about the nature of things	To trace a problem to its source & develop ingenious ways to resolve it
6	To learn how to resolve our fears & develop trust	To face our worst fears about the work and continue with it anyway
7	To use our many gifts in a way that is joyful but focused	To use new gifts to make the final result something special
8	To achieve mastery without ignoring our debt to others & to life	To create a masterpiece that recognizes the contributions made at each previous stage
9	To allow our natural receptivity to give rise to imaginative ideas & new possibilities	To let go of the old and become receptive to the new

Why Link Personality with Process

Here are some of the key reasons why it's advantageous for those of us who work with the personality enneagram to envision the enneagram types as points in a transformational process.

First, *it helps us understand how the enneagram types serve a positive function* in life (because each one corresponds to an essential step in transformational change).

Second, *it gives us a more powerful way to work with the enneagram* because it brings together two existing enneagram models, each of which has the potential to inform the other.

Third, *it underscores the value of differentiated functioning* (individuality) by showing us that each point in a transformational process is necessary and useful.

Fourth, *it gives us deeper insights* into the nature of the nine personality types, so that we understand (a) why each type has particular characteristics and (b) why it occupies a particular position on the enneagram circle. We discover, for example:

- why Ones tend to be focused and serious
  (they have to develop ethical ideals with lasting value)

- why Twos seek friends and form social networks
  (they must transform ideals into projects that real people can relate to)

- why Threes are doers and achievers
  (they need to determine what works & what doesn't)

- why Fours feel pulled into the depths
  (they have to delve beneath superficial images & initial impressions)

- why Fives revere knowledge
  (they have to understand the essential nature of what is going on)

- why Sixes are dutiful but ambivalent
  (they must strive to counter fear & doubt with faith & service)

- why Sevens tend to have many gifts but lack focus
  (they have been exposed to too many possibilities to settle down yet)

- why Eights have such "big" energy
  (they have to embody the completeness of life)

- why Nines seem to exude peace but can seem overly passive
  (they are in a state of "beingness" & receptivity)

Stability versus Fixation

Seeing the "whys" of each type gives us an alternative way to think of the nine enneagram points of view: not as nine points of psychological fixation but as nine fixed points (stages) in a transformational journey. Such fixed points of reference are necessary to stabilize gains and prepare for the next stage. In the same way, our enneagram point of view is necessary if we're to achieve a stable psychological reference point.

Having a stable point of view provides us with a practical framework for individual development, a framework which is the psychological equivalent of our body's skeleton. Just as our skeleton provides us with a structure that organizes the body, our type provides us with a structure that organizes the psyche. It's a stabilizing influence that's invaluable for maintaining psychic integrity.

Life is dynamic and ever-changing. Without a stable point of reference, change can seem like chaos; clarity quickly degenerates into confusion. It becomes difficult to maintain our equilibrium in dynamic situations—to be fully present in the moment or to bring our creative abilities to the peak of perfection. It's even more difficult to handle the destabilizing effects of transformational spiritual work.

Transformation always involves both *transcendence* (the ability to move beyond the physical plane) and *immanence* (the ability to anchor spiritual energy in the physical plane). The two can seem like opposites, because one focuses on spirit and the other on matter. But the two actually work together: groundedness in life facilitates transcendence while transcendence gives meaning and purpose to life. So the two aren't opposites, but complements (like yin and yang).

Most enneagram work emphasizes transcendence—specifically, the transcendence of our enneagram type. But if we seek to transcend our type without appreciating how it helps us live life on earth, then we're missing half the equation. We need to understand that one does not preclude the other—that *we can transcend our type while also fully embodying it*, where *embodying the type* means understanding its nature, appreciating its benefits, and being open to its challenges. As a Sufi master once observed, "to reach the stars, our feet must be firmly planted on the ground."

Being grounded also tends to inhibit the development of arrogance and narcissism, because it enables us to see the importance of ordinary virtues like taking responsibility, accepting feedback, and admitting dumb mistakes (instead of pretending they didn't happen!). Groundedness also helps us laugh at our foibles and forgive other people when they hurt our feelings. We discover that we don't have to become a "spiritual superstar" in order to feel good about ourselves and our lives.

In the next (and last) chapter, we explore this idea further, exploring ways to become more integrated, attuned, and creative—and to do it without necessarily needing to transcend the boundaries of our type.

One Last Note

Please don't get the idea that mapping the personality enneagram onto the process enneagram is meant to imply that types with lower numbers (1, 2, 3, etc.) are somehow less evolved, advanced, etc., than those with higher numbers (7, 8, 9), because the former are "just beginning" and latter are "at the end." Although we draw the enneagram as a circle, it's actually more like a spiral. Any of us can be anywhere on that spiral.

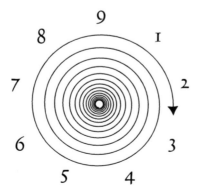

The Enneagram
as a Living System

The best thing about working with the enneagram from a positive perspective is that it really brings the system to life. It opens our eyes to new ways of working with the system, to whole new vistas that inspire the imagination. In this chapter, we'll look at some of these innovative approaches.

Bringing the system to life allows us to return to the spirit of G. I. Gurdjieff's original teachings on the enneagram, teachings rooted in the idea that the enneagram is a dynamic system—so much so that Gurdjieff likened it to a perpetual motion machine. I prefer to borrow a metaphor from ecology and call it a *living system*.

A living system possesses three key attributes: differentiation, communication, and definition. *Differentiation* is necessary so that different parts of the system can do different things; *communication* is necessary so that these elements can exchange information; and *definition* is necessary to delineate the outer boundaries of the system—to define it as a single entity (a whole). To the extent that those outer boundaries are permeable (like a cell wall), each system can participate as a cell within the body of yet another, larger system. In addition, its permeable boundaries enable it to exchange information with other systems at a similar level of complexity.

This is how a living system works—a living system like the enneagram. The structure of the enneagram is composed of all three elements: differentiated parts (the nine types), lines of energy exchange (the inner lines), and an outer ring that delineates the boundaries of the system (the circle).

This kind of living system goes by many names, depending on the field in question (see chart below). What's interesting about the fields listed below is that most of them are *emergent*—that is, they are based on an image of life that is just now emerging into view. Because this image is rooted in the insights of modern (quantum) physics, it can be called a *quantum* view of life, one in which such concepts as simple complexity, order-within-chaos, and other puzzling paradoxes are the norm, not the exception.

This quantum view is creating a revolution in the way people think, although the process has been slow to get off the ground because these quantum ideas are too alien to easily assimilate. But this situation is beginning to change. Many points of view that once seemed irreconcilable (for example, those of science and spirituality) are beginning

Ways to Describe a Living System

AREA OF STUDY	SYSTEM TYPE
Quantum theory	quantum system
Systems theory	open system
Chaos theory	self-organizing system
Complexity theory	emergent system
Field theory	intelligent field
Artificial intelligence	natural system
Biology	self-organizing system
Ecology	ecosystem
Archetypal psychology	archetypal system
Psycho-spiritual psychology	transformative system
Positive psychology	life-affirming system
Family systems	open-boundary system
Transpersonal psychology	self-transcending system
Integral theory	holonic system
Esoteric theory	mystical or numinous system
Gestalt psychology	holistic system
Humanistic psychology	self-actualizing system

to converge. Paradoxical findings—such as the fact that light is both a particle and a wave—are no longer seen as anomalous eccentricities, and even research into such topics as life after death is beginning to make an impact on both the popular and scientific culture. Such developments are bringing home the truth that there really *are* different dimensions of reality, each with its own properties and laws.

Even so, in the psychological sense, most of us still live in a Newtonian world. We still visualize ourselves as material creatures trudging around in a mechanical, three-dimensional universe, not as balls of energy whirling about in a marvelously paradoxical 11-dimensional multiverse. But this viewpoint is changing, because it *must*—we are in the midst of a revolutionary paradigm shift that is going to change the way we view ourselves, our lives, and our world.

The enneagram has a role to play in this revolution. Why? Because it's a system which exemplifies both the paradoxes and power of the quantum paradigm. So far, it has yet to realize its revolutionary potential, because it's seldom taught from a revolutionary perspective. It's a powerful system, but a system whose power has yet to be fully utilized (we could compare it to a brand-new computer equipped with dated software).

So my purpose in this chapter is to present examples of how to see the enneagram from a quantum perspective, as an open system that is dynamic, alive, and non-dualistic. In systems theory, an open system is one which is able to maintain its integrity while freely exchanging information with its environment. Because of its openness and ability to maintain its equilibrium, it's not subject to the laws of entropy. So it can continue to evolve as long as it can remain in balance and acquire new sources of energy.

In contrast to open systems are *closed systems,* which are static, unreceptive to new information, and unable to generate new energy on their own. Because of their rigidity and inability to easily adapt to changing environmental conditions, they have a limited life span.

Not surprisingly, most of us prefer open systems. This is because they tend to foster happier families, better work situations, and closer-knit communities. Closed systems may limp along for a while, but eventually they all succumb to entropy, so they are like a giant watch that has been wound up once but which is gradually running down. Open systems don't run down like this, because they're both self-generative and improvisational. They thrive on new ideas and methodologies.

It's because the enneagram is an open system that it has the power to help us become both more balanced and more energized. In this chapter, I give several examples of how this works, how the enneagram can help us to

- resolve stubborn conflicts
- find our path in life
- enhance our creativity

In brief, the enneagram helps us *resolve conflicts* by introducing us to an integrative "three-point" perspective which helps us reframe conflict situations in a way that facilitates their resolution. It helps us *find new direction* by acquainting us with the paths particularly well-suited to the temperament of our type. And it helps us *live more creatively* by enabling us to understand how the limitations imposed by our type are actually crucibles for creative refinement.

Using the Enneagram to Resolve Conflicts

Conflict resolution is a big job for all of us, whether we're a diplomat trying to prevent a war or just an ordinary person trying to hold a job and get along better with our friends and family. Whatever our situation in life, we can all benefit from understanding what to do when conflict arises. This is true whether the conflict involves outer relationships or the flow of our inner energy.

A whole book could be written about using the enneagram for conflict resolution. What I'm going to talk about here is a basic paradigm for working with conflict situations based on the energy and geometry of the enneagram—what I call a *third-point approach* or *third-point thinking*. Using this approach, it's possible to shift the way we think about conflict situations. When the energy shifts, the whole situation looks different. And new possibilities for resolution emerge.

This model of conflict resolution is based on Gurdjieff's Law of Three. The Law of Three is based on the esoteric principle that life can be conceptualized as having a threefold nature, such that, for any dichotomy we observe in life, there exists a "hidden third point" that

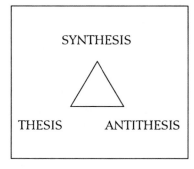

tends to reconcile, harmonize, or create common ground between two diametrically opposing points of view.

Gurdjieff referred to this third point as a *third force* (in keeping with his rather muscular way of speaking). One of his main goals was to demonstrate how the geometry of the enneagram embodies this principle. This is not difficult (at least on a basic level) because the third-force thinking is essentially triangular in nature, and the triangle is such a prominent feature in the enneagram.

The Law of Three may sound abstract, but it's a powerful concept with many applications, as we'll see. It gives us a framework for problem solving that's not only practical but integrative in outlook. This means that it tends to generate "win-win"—rather than "win-lose"—solutions. And this is why it's such an effective problem-solving approach.

Anyone with a background in philosophy will recognize this trifold model as basically the same thing as Hegel's thesis/antithesis/synthesis model, which sets forth the idea that for any two opposing forces, there's a third force that can bring about a synthesis. Apparently, although Hegel set forth the model, he did little to develop it further. By the time Gurdjieff came along almost a century later, the third-point approach still hadn't been much developed, as Gurdjieff was quick to point out. This is true even today. As a result, three-point thinking remains a hazy idea whose potential has yet to be fully realized.

To understand why, we first have to look at the usual way that most of us envision conflict situations: from an oppositional or *dualistic* perspective. Dualism has been around in Western culture for a long time (for centuries, if not *millennia*), so it's deeply embedded in our thinking.

SYNTHESIS

THESIS   ANTITHESIS

Dualistic approaches are based on the idea that everything in life "comes in twos": we have male vs. female, black vs. white, good vs. bad—well, you get the picture. When dualism prevails, reality gets carved up into neat little dichotomous boxes that always seem to be incompatible with one another. So instead of promoting a "win-win" way of thinking, dualism promotes a "win-lose" approach. Life becomes an "us versus them" proposition, where nobody wants to be a loser, so we all fight tooth and nail for the high ground in life.

Dualism does not encourage cooperation or integration. It encourages *competition*—not the healthy competition we see in healthy Threes, but the cutthroat, survival-of-the-fittest competition driven by the belief that our win must be the product of somebody else's loss.

Many people intuitively sense that this kind of thinking does not create a happy life, yet have a hard time getting out of a dualistic mind-set. Like any powerful, long-standing belief system, dualism is pervasive. It's hard to really grasp how pervasive it is—and how profoundly it affects our perceptions, judgments, and acts. We might reject the idea of dualism and yet still respond to many problems in daily life by framing them in dualistic ("either/or") terms, thereby limiting our options.

Sometimes it's easier to see how this works by looking at examples in films or on TV. For example, take the hokey (but still useful) made-for-TV movie plot that starts out by showing us a divorced or separated couple who are continually picking silly fights that could easily be avoided if either partner were willing to cooperate instead of argue. This dynamic is obvious to anybody who watches them interact. But the couple themselves seems clueless.

However, they have a child, which is usually why they're still talking at all. The child hates the fighting and becomes convinced that he's the source of the problem. So he decides to run away. Usually, the adults are so distracted by their own troubles that they fail to notice he's gone until it's way too late to trace his steps.

When the two adults realize that he's gone, they suddenly wake up and smell the coffee. They realize that he has probably disappeared because of *them*—because they were unwilling to resolve their differences. Now they have an incentive to do so: their child is in danger, and they are responsible.

It's the shock of this discovery that shakes them loose from dualistic thinking. It also creates in them a powerful desire to change the situation, to break out of their dualistic deadlock. This desire becomes so powerful that it brooks no disagreement. Both parents unite to affirm that the child

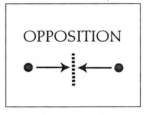

is safe and will be found. They pour all their energy into this idea and remove all their energy from alternative possibilities. They also tirelessly work toward their goal, marshalling all their creative resources in the process. In so doing, they completely reframe their way of looking at themselves, their partner, and life. They feel gratitude for what they once took for granted.

Whatever the outcome of the story (which is usually predictably positive in made-for-TV movies), one thing is certain: the former adversaries are no longer enemies. They've gone through a life-altering experience that's managed to transform their relationship in a way that's taken them out of their oppositional deadlock.

How did they do it? Via third-point thinking: by taking all the energy they once devoted to opposing one another and channeling it toward a new, more constructive goal. They made the big shift from dualistic thinking to integrative thinking, from *opposition* to *integration*.

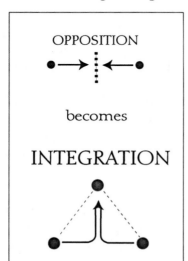

The above example is hokey because it's too cut and dried to capture the complexity involved in a real-life situation. In real life, bad things *do* happen to good people. And some of them are tragic. But many bad situations can be avoided or greatly mitigated by third-point (integrative) thinking, because it's an approach in which we realize that *the solution is always present in the problem.* It's just a matter of locating it.

It's hard to overestimate the transformative power of seeing life from a solution-oriented perspective. This integrative shift has the power to rescue us from any number of deadlocked situations, big and small. Whenever a problem or conflict arises, we automatically start seeking its solution (rather than focusing on the difficulty of the problem).

The enneagram supports this move away from negative dualism because it shows us that the Law of Three is intrinsic to life. It also shows us the nature of our inner selves: our core motivation. When we combine an understanding of the nature of life with an understanding of the self, we have the basis for living a more fulfilled life—a life based on what Buddhists call "right action."

Right action is possible only when we're able to integrate all aspects of a situation in a way that permits us to transcend linear thinking. It's the result of a state of mind in which problems lose their power to mentally defeat us; we see them as challenges to be met (or if we're on a lofty enough spiritual perch, as illusions to be dispelled). Once we're in that frame of mind, it can be surprisingly easy to "reverse engineer" a solution. Really big difficulties may require more time

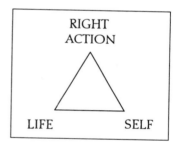

and energy to resolve, but 90% of the little conflicts we experience on an everyday basis will simply dissolve once we cease to fuel them with oppositional thinking.

This is not the same thing as putting our heads in the sand and pretending that problems don't exist. It's exactly the opposite. Third-point awareness requires us to be present in the moment—present enough to notice what's actually going on. Being present is important, because we need every bit of information we can get if we're going to unearth an optimal solution.

Third-point thinking is what skillful mediators utilize when they encounter two groups whose differences seem irreconcilable. They instinctively know how to talk to everybody in the room in a way that helps them become aware of shared goals and common interests. If nothing else, a skilled mediator can get warring factions to see one another's basic humanity. Once this happens, some sort of reconciliation usually becomes possible.

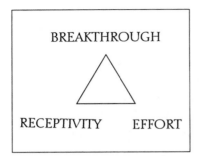

BREAKTHROUGH

RECEPTIVITY   EFFORT

A third-point approach is what innovative thinkers and creators use when they work. Whenever they run into a problem, they grapple with it with such focus and tenacity that they eventually break through to a new level of understanding. Usually, this integrative understanding comes to them when they finally disengage from the struggle (usually because they're exhausted). They let go of everything and stop thinking about the problem. Perhaps they fall asleep. When they wake up (or perhaps when they dream), the solution magically appears. Maximum effort plus maximum receptivity combine to create a new discovery or an original work of art.

Effective prayer is another third-point process, because it involves pondering the problem, reflecting on our own actions, and cultivating receptivity. Prayer moves us out of "either/or" thinking (which makes us feel caught between various awful possibilities) toward "both/and" thinking (which is uplifting and mood-elevating). This shift in consciousness creates the conditions necessary for something positive to take place. Meditation is similar in nature, except that it's even more open-ended.

These examples demonstrate how third-point thinking helps us transform conflicts or problems into opportunities to experience a more coherent level of awareness. Qualities that facilitate this transformation include sensitivity, tolerance, presence, relatedness, discernment, spontaneity, persistence, originality, and fairness. These qualities can be cultivated by any of us, but each one comes more naturally to some people than others. Why is this? Because (in case you didn't notice), there's one for each of the nine types! (Can you guess which quality goes with which type? See the enneagram on p. 176 for the answer.)

The enneagram is clearly a system based on three-point thinking; it shows

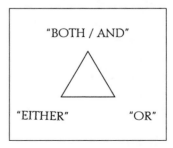

"BOTH / AND"

"EITHER"   "OR"

up everywhere we look. There are nine types that can be arranged in many 3 x 3 configurations, each of which show us how any two opposing points can be resolved by looking to the energy of a third point.

For example, we have three energy centers (Head, Heart, and Gut). Many dramas both in film and in real life are based on conflicts between two people whose types are located in different centers. To resolve their differences, they have to find common ground—and this usually involves bringing in the energy of our third (least preferred) center.

We can see this scenario unfold in the movie *Awakenings*, set in 1969, where a shy Five physician (Robin Williams) uses the then-new drug L-dopa to awaken long-time victims of sleeping sickness, including Robert De Niro (a Five-ish Eight). Doctor and patient find common ground only when they both get up the courage to open their hearts (to access the energy of the Heart Center). De Niro does this when he falls in love; Williams when he realizes the love he feels for his patients (and the pain he experiences when he begins to realize that the effects of the drug are only temporary).

Another example is the film *Moonlight Mile* with Dustin Hoffman and Susan Sarandon, where Hoffman plays an anxious Head type (a Six) and Sarandon is a tough-but-tender Heart type (a Self-preservation Four). They're both mourning the death of their only daughter, whom we never meet. The one we *do* get to know is her blank-faced but agreeable fiance, a Nine (Jake Gyllenhaal). Hoffman and Sarandon keep themselves from falling to pieces by projecting all their hopes and dreams onto the hapless Nine, who obligingly allows it— at least for a while. His challenge is to is break free from their projections; their challenge is to find within themselves the groundedness (that is, the Gut Center energy) they need to get through this crisis on their own. Fortunately, all three characters eventually manage to overcome their various challenges, becoming stronger and more confident as a result.

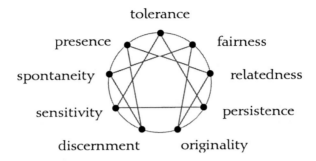

tolerance

presence

fairness

spontaneity

relatedness

sensitivity

persistence

discernment   originality

Qualities Facilitating Third-Point Awareness

To see lots of real-life examples, tune in to *Wife Swap*, a reality TV show that seeks out people who are diametrically opposed in viewpoint and "swaps" the wives of both families for two weeks. The swap inevitably brings together people who have very different lifestyles. It's a fascinating program for anyone interested in the enneagram, because many of the classic conflicts experienced by people of different types, subtypes, and centers show up in spades. Compulsively clean Ones are plopped into messy Seven homes where people just want to have fun. Overly intellectual Fives have to put up with overly ambitious Threes who are busy eight days a week. Or primly conventional Sixes confront the strange idiosyncrasies of quirky artistic Fours.

The participants bravely strive to overcome their differences during the two-week window allotted for that purpose. It's a tough proposition for most of them. What's amazing to see is just how many of the participants actually manage to pull it off (despite a lot of grousing along the way). Most of them actually manage to make long-term changes that bring greater balance to their family culture, something that's only possible when people transcend their oppositional way of thinking.

The most powerful work I've seen with the enneagram is grounded in the same kind of integrative approach. But this kind of work only becomes possible when we stop using it to reinforce dualistic ideas (like the idea that self can be meaningfully divided into two separate compartments, labeled "ego" and "essence").

So one of my goals is to liberate the enneagram from its current dualistic paradigm. Just imagine what it might be like to use the power of the enneagram not just to identify blind spots and defenses but to find a greater sense of purpose and direction in life. That's our focus in the next section.

Discovering Our Path in Life

Jack Kornfeld once wrote a book called *A Path with Heart* about his spiritual journey through life. Kornfeld is a Theravadan monk and meditation teacher, yet his book is not about transcending everyday reality. It's about making life worthwhile *right where we are.* He speaks of the value of seeing life itself as a temple, a place where we can develop all the qualities we need for happiness: mindfulness, healing, emotional integration, service, acceptance, community, and ethics.

It's easy to think that finding a path is just for people on a spiritual quest. But this isn't true. We all want to live the kind of life that really suits us—the kind of life that can bring us happiness and fulfillment.

A cynic may argue that this is not at all what most people want—that what they want is power, prestige, attention, property, or pleasure. But I would disagree. People chase after such things only because they don't know what else to chase after—what else might make them happy. Or because they're convinced that what would *really* make them happy is unattainable. They may have tried hard to achieve what they wanted and met with repeated frustration. Finally, they gave up and settled for a cheap substitute.

But none of us start out that way as kids. We

just get sidetracked somewhere along the way. To get back on track, we need to harmonize our inner nature with our outer lives—to bring the two together in a way that ensures a proper fit. When this happens, life begins to lose its arbitrary, random quality and begins to reveal its subtle inner order. We start to see that we each have a role to play in this order: a role that is exactly right for us as individuals. Out of this understanding arises the intuitive awareness of where to go and what to do. We begin to discover what people have called our *vocation, calling, destiny, life path, life's work,* or *dharma.*

Of all these terms, I like the word *dharma* the best because it has many subtle qualities that convey what finding Kornfeld's path with heart is all about. It's a Sanskrit word that is not easily translated, but it roughly means *duty* or *service.* Dharma has also been described as *that which upholds and supports* or as *a virtuous path.*

So finding the dharma is not just about finding the right work (as in finding our calling, vocation, or life's work) or about having some extra-special task to accomplish in life (as in "fulfilling our destiny"). While dharma encompasses such things, it's a more basic idea. Even the term *dharma* is more unassuming in tone. It conveys the sense that although we all have a particular role to play in life, it's not because we are special in the egotistical sense. It's simply because we're human.

The idea that dharma is "that which upholds and supports" suggests that there is an implicit order or structure to life, and that each of us has a role to play in upholding that order. This means that *life matters*—and that *we matter,* too. Understanding this truth brings dignity and worth to even the smallest tasks in life. It helps us do our best, even in trying situations.

While dharma may be about service, it's not about mindlessly following orders. Fulfilling the dharma is not like following a set of instructions—it's more like actively participating in the gradual unfoldment of a very open-ended plan, but the kind of plan that has a certain fateful quality to it.

Dharma initially exists only as a potential awaiting fulfillment. It's like raw talent or an innate predisposition that's awaiting cultivation. The basic blueprint is there but it's mostly blank. If we're to fill in the blanks, we have to recognize our dharmic potential and actively participate in its fulfillment.

But all too often, we not only fail to participate but actually resist the unfolding of dharma. Why? Because we're afraid to follow such an open-ended plan, scared of what might happen (or fail to happen). So we over-control our lives, unaware that life is designed in such a way that we can afford to let go—that there is a "safety net" that will catch us if we fall. But we only make this discovery if we get brave enough to allow ourselves to fall sometimes. If we cling too hard to our pre-existing plans, we never get to see just how synchronistic life can be.

This was the main message of a little book I recently read, *Things Will Get As Good As You Can Stand*. Its author, Laura Doyle, says that one of the main reasons why life so often disappoints us is that we

ourselves block the way, becoming our own worst enemy. We say we want fulfillment, but then we're not willing to let life support our dreams. We hold so tightly to those dreams that they never become realities.

The book title also hints at the idea that some of us aren't quite convinced that we *deserve* a better life. Doyle says we do. But we can't move forward as long as we lack faith in ourselves.

I agree. It's why I emphasize the positive traits of the enneagram types—because they help us see our gifts and potentials. This understanding helps us appreciate those gifts and use them wisely. It also helps us appreciate the positive potential of the other eight types, which fosters a sense of mutual respect and cooperation.

Some people are afraid that focusing on our gifts (much less developing them) might cause ego inflation. But if we develop our gifts with the goal of fulfilling the dharma—this is not likely to inflate the ego, because dharma is service-focused, not ego-focused. The fulfillment of dharma occurs in the larger context of the family, the community, and life. It entails the understanding that personal fulfillment necessarily involves the satisfying of one's obligations in life (remember, the word *dharma* means *duty*). So finding the dharma means determining the nature of those duties and cultivating the willingness to fulfill them. That sort of path is not likely to produce ego inflation.

The bigger problem is not actually ego inflation, it's lack of interest—lack of interest in the whole idea of living a life focused on duty. The very word *duty* makes most of us wince, probably because we've lost the understanding of what real duty entails, having relegated it to the wasteland of unpopular ideas. We think that duty is about adopting some sort of grimly puritanical way of life or doing things for the sake of propriety. But it's more about cultivating a way of life that's in harmony with both our own nature and our environment. It involves responsibility, but it need not be joyless or unhappy. In fact, just the opposite is true.

The enneagram gives us a more accurate picture of how dharma actually works by helping us discover not only truths about ourselves, but truths about how we fit into the larger scheme of things (based on the position of our point of view on the circle). It shows us ways to get along with the other eight types, so we can be in "right relationship" more of the time. And it shows us how to use our particular talents to serve others, so we can make the world a better place to live.

With this understanding, we don't need to de-emphasize type-related gifts, for fear of developing some kind of narcissistic preoccupation. Narcissism is a by-product of seeing ourselves out of context, as separate from life. It does not arise when we really understand ourselves and our relationship with life.

Many of us used to think that we had to kill the personality in order to be a spiritual person. But this idea is clearly outdated. Spiritual teacher Ram Dass remembers the era when ego death was the goal of spiritual aspirants, especially in the West. But he recently remarked that forty years of spiritual practice have not made the slightest dent in his personality. Despite all the changes in his life over the years, he still has the same personality quirks he had when he was young. The only difference, he says, is that now he relates to them differently. His personality quirks are no longer the enemy; they're just *there,* part of his inner landscape. (I would go even further, saying that personality is actually the vehicle through which we live out the dharma, especially if we expand our notion of personality to include deeper aspects of individuality. It's the vehicle through which we make a contribution to life, through which we anchor spirit in matter. So the more we know about it, the more intelligently we can work with it.)

How does the enneagram support the fulfillment of dharma? In a number of ways:

- by describing our core motivations, gifts, and vulnerabilities
- by facilitating better relationships
- by showing us typical ways that the energy of each type shows up in everyday life

It can also reveal the archetypal paths, roles, and themes associated with each type—themes that show us how dharma can manifest in our lives. I've listed some of them on the next two pages.

Archetypal Paths, Roles & Themes by Enneagram Type

1	Persevering Pioneer, Courageous Settler, Sober Citizen, Strict Disciplinarian, Meticulous Craftsman, Grammarian, Precise Copy Editor, Parsimonious Spender, Monk, Nun, Ascetic, Renunciate, Evangelist, Proselytizer, Missionary, Puritan, Confessor, Mentor, Demonstrator, Protester, Reformer, Advocate, Rule-maker, Judge, Impartial Lawgiver, Jurist, Lawyer, Priest, Spiritual Hierophant, Chief Justice, Religious Educator, Mother Superior, Chief Examiner, Exacting Auditor, Impartial Advocate, Parliamentarian, Old Testament Prophet, Ardent Arbiter, "Miss Manners"
2	Doting Mother, Devoted Caregiver, Content Homemaker, Home Cook, Caring Nurse, Fairy Godmother, Willing Helper, Gracious Giver, Sympathetic Listener, Shrewd Matchmaker, Inquisitive Busybody, Martyr, Self-sacrificer, Rescuer, Diva, Maestro, Helpmate, Partner, Lover, Flirt, Romancer, Seducer, Femme Fatale, Casanova, Playboy, Harlot, Vestal Virgin, Holy Innocent, Saint, Devotee, Diplomat, Ambassador, Friend, Social Networker, Humanitarian, Event Hostess, Social Smoother, Behind-the-scenes Organizer, Power Behind the Throne, Hidden Partner, Bleeding Heart
3	Achiever, Careerist, Adapter, Go-getter, Pragmatist, "Type A," Comeback Kid, Big Fish in a Small Pond, Public Personality, Aspirant, Superstar, Popular Hero, Sex Goddess, Glamour Queen, Fashion Plate, Model, Manicured Professional, Media Sensation, Masculine Ideal, Feminine Ideal, Venus, Team Leader, Office Seeker, Opinion Leader, Politician, Head of the Class, Valedictorian, First Among Equals, Credentialed Consultant, Lobbyist, Prestige Elite Member, PR Expert, Public Relations Genius, Spin Doctor, Glosser-over, Master Deal-maker
4	Deep Sea Diver, Bohemian, Artisan, Craftsman, Gypsy, Weaver, Originator, Fierce Individualist, Independent Learner, Wounded Healer, Wordsmith, Spiritual Gambler, Edge-walker, Dramatist, Artist, Poet, Method Actor, Writer, Novelist, Goth, Moth to the Flame, Fierce Competitor, Romantic Rival, Intense Seeker, Misunderstood Artist, Damsel in Distress, Abandoned Child, Drama Queen/King, Seeker, Pundit, Social Critic, Rebel Without A Cause, Feng Shui Consultant, Commentator, Designer, Pained Isolate, Social Muckraker, Alienated Idealist, Courageous Confronter

5	Thinker, Intellectual, Genius, Philosopher, Puzzle-solver, Observer, Tinkerer, Theorist, Inventor, Scholar, Intellectual, Hermit, Nerd, Recluse, Spy, Sleuth, Alchemist, Scientist, Investigator, Private Detective, Undercover Operative, Internet Wizard, Chess Player, Photographer, Recognized Expert, Teacher, Professor, Impersonal Guide, Bodhisattva, Iconoclast, Etymologist, Myth Collector, Anthropologist, Arcane Expert, Wise Man or Woman, Tribal Healer, Shaman, Witch Doctor
6	Intuitive, Psychic, Sensitive, Worrier, Shy Welcomer, Family Preserver, Faithful Companion, Concerned Parent, Loyal Employee, Host or Hostess, Homemaker, Scrapper, Protector, Debater, Underdog Fighter, Warrior, Soldier of Fortune, Tender Defender, Battlefield Medic, Beauty Queen, Miss America, Braveheart, Sensitive Creator, Aesthetic Appreciator, Idealistic Lover, Shy Sensualist, Steward, Dutiful Server, Conserver of the Social Order, Historian, Archivist, Recorder, Volunteer, Community Builder, Committee Worker, Prosecutor, Law Enforcement Officer, Brave Firefighter, Reluctant Whistle Blower, True Believer
7	Bon Vivant, Renaissance Man, Magical Child, Fun Parent, Pastry Chef, "Good Life" Aficionado, Family Entertainer, Entrepreneur, Interior Designer, Home Improver, Versatile Generalist, Self-improvement Junkie, Idea Spinner, Artless Charmer, Dance-away Lover, Shameless Hedonist, Space Cadet, Comic, Mimic, Hippie, Dreamer, Artist, Trickster, Vagabond, Wanderer, Juggler, Fool, Gambler, Jack of All Trades, Raconteur, Troubadour, Idealist, Visionary, Utopian, Futurist, Planner, Architect, Herald, Courier, Networker, Innovator, Communicator, Trendsetter, Jet-setter
8	Born Leader, Master, Heavyweight, Strong Man, Strong Silent Type, Weight Lifter, Mountain Man, Mountain Mama, Force of Nature, Survivalist, Pillar of Strength, God or Goddess, Guru, Champion, Gunslinger, Knight Errant, Hero, Honor-bound Avenger, Pirate King, Martial Artist, Hunter or Huntress, Patriarch, King, Emperor, Ruler, Autocrat, CEO, Boss, Leader of the Pack, Mafia Don, Military Commander, Chieftain, Tactician, Strategist, Commander in Chief, Tough-love Parent, Dominant Friend, One of the Boys, A Real Pal
9	Mediator, Meditator, Practical Person, Reliable Worker, Sensible Thinker, Nature Lover, Putterer, Peasant, Serf, Slave, Nomad, Herdsman, Crop Picker, Gardener, Landscaper, Tribe Member, Cowhand, Gardener, Herbalist, Manual Laborer, Servant, Retainer, Natural Mystic, Fantasy Spinner, Dreamer, Storyteller, Enjoyer of Pleasure, Devotee, Tabula Rasa, Nature Worshipper, Animal Lover, Lover of Love, Group Participant, Community Member, Natural Mediator, Harmonizer, Blender, Go-between, Peacemaker, Consensus Builder, Facilitator, Coach, Cooperator, Referee

Creative Living with the Enneagram

If finding our path is about setting our lives on a long-term course, creative living is about something much more immediate: being *present in the moment,* present in a way that helps us stay in tune with our surroundings. This can be tricky, because it requires us to balance our desire for freedom with the need to adjust to limitation.

The moment, after all, imposes many limitations on us. It brings us beautiful sunsets, moments of triumph, and sexual ecstasy, but it also brings us traffic jams, bad bosses, and screaming toddlers. Creative living means learning to deal with the good and the bad, especially the bad! (Nobody seems to need lessons in how to appreciate a good meal or a walk on the beach.)

Creative people may not have perfect equanimity in difficult situations, but they do seem to have a certain knack for getting through the bad bits without becoming totally discombobulated. At the same time, they know how to transform commonplace experiences into something memorable, even with limited time, energy, or resources. They don't need a perfect situation to work their magic; they work with whatever materials are at hand.

The question is: How do they do it?

In *Free Play: Improvisation in Life and Art,* author Stephen Nachmanovich says it's by learning how to see life as art, and by using limitations as a source of creative inspiration. He notes that we create art by constraining some values so that others may vary more freely. From this viewpoint, limitations act as the crucible for creation. They're not only helpful, but essential, because without such limits, "art is not possible."

To think of limitation as a source of inspiration may seem strange, but it's actually a variation of third-point thinking where the nature of the limits determines the type of art that is possible. No form of artistic expression is free from limits; in fact, the greatest art forms are often those that impose the greatest limits.

For example, say I want to write a poem. The easiest thing to write is free-form verse, which has very few limits.

> All I have to do,
> Is arrange my words like so:
> A poem is born.

This may not be great poetry, but it is a poem of sorts. If I want to rhyme the lines, that adds another level of constraint:

> All I have to do
> Is arrange my words like so:
> Now my poem looks poetic,
> Could I sell it for some dough?

If I want to write a sonnet, that's going to take a *lot* more work. (Don't worry, I'm not going to attempt an example...perhaps the reader would like to give it a try?)

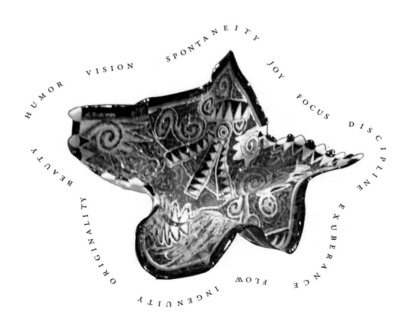

A living tree or a work of art?

The point is that free-form verse has very few constraints, rhymed verse has more, and complex forms such as sonnets or *haiku* have many more. Most of us would agree that composing *haiku* requires tremendous focus and perseverance; so it is with all great art.

Limits give us an arena, area, discipline, container, or field within which we can work. They define the boundaries of our project, imposing constraints that we must be prepared to accept if we want to accomplish anything significant. For example, if I want to get married, I have to sacrifice the autonomy I have as a single person. If I want an athletic scholarship to college, I have to sacrifice free time so I can go to practice. If I yearn to write a novel or dance in the ballet, I have to accept the artistic limits imposed by those disciplines.

Having too little limitation is like having unlimited amounts of money when we're young—it makes us spoiled, dependent, and uncreative. We never learn how to properly appreciate money. We never learn how to budget. We never experience the genuine pleasure of finding a bargain or the pride of opening our first paycheck, knowing we can make it on our own.

So the absence of limitation is not very good for creative living, because it puts us out of touch both with reality and with ourselves. Then there's no joy, no gratitude, no sense of personal satisfaction. We just float in space, waiting for something to happen. This is probably why boredom is such a problem for the super-rich, jet-setting elite. We ordinary mortals envy them their privilege without realizing the price they pay.

The optimal situation is having enough limitation to give us some sense of connectedness to life but not so much that we feel like we can't move. We need the right balance between these two extremes. We also need to be aware of the nature of the limits; this helps us stay out of hot water but it also helps us bounce off those limits in creative ways. I had a friend with unpopular political views who served on a student council. He could never get anybody to listen to his ideas. The group would just "call the question" before he could air his views. So he became an expert on Robert's Rules of Order, which made him realize that the group was continually violating their own rules without realizing it. After that, any time they wanted to arbitrarily shut him up, he would cite some obscure but valid rule, and they would have to let him continue. Knowing the rules also got him a lot of respect in the group. Although he didn't manage to win the whole group over to his way of thinking, he did manage to raise their level of consciousness; people became much more careful about what they said and did.

My friend's approach relied not only on knowing a set of limits but also on understanding how to use that knowledge for creative purposes. That's what the best lawyers also do—they combine a knowledge of the law with the ability to think outside of the box.

Creative real estate agents use a similar approach when negotiating a house sale. They have to find a way to bring buyer and seller together, making both parties feel good about the deal. The agents also have to alert them to the realities of the market so the buyers aren't looking for their dream house when they only have enough money for a starter home—and the sellers aren't artificially inflating the selling price, based on idiosyncratic improvements that are of little value to anybody else (like an outdoor hot tub installed *inside* a home—this is a real example!). Trying to make a match between two parties with such different priorities requires considerable presence, flexibility, and originality.

So creative thinking isn't just for artists—it's for anybody. It requires us to understand two things: the boundary conditions for our work and the ability to use those conditions as a source of inspiration.

How do we do this? By cultivating the kind of character traits that foster a creative approach to living, for example, discernment, self-discipline, playfulness, humor, resourcefulness, and imagination. These qualities will always stand us in good stead, whether we're writing a play, designing a building, creating play activities for toddlers, or surviving a plane crash in the wilderness. All these scenarios impose limitations that demand a creative yet disciplined response. We see these kinds of situations dramatized in films like *Life is Beautiful*, *What Dreams May Come*, *My Left Foot*, *Magnolia*, *Bicentennial Man*, or *Steel Magnolias*. What such films have in common is the inspirational theme that, despite the vicissitudes of life, it's always possible to find a creative response suitable for the situation (even when the situation is painfully limiting).

Limitation is also a natural part of our physical and mental make-up. The physical body itself imposes a number of limitations on our perception and cognition. The brain is a "limited capacity processor," meaning it is amazingly constrained in the amount of information it can process at any given moment; scientists tell us that the maximum is between 7 – 9 separate bits. Recent research shows that for most of us, the limits are more like 3 – 6 bits.

A related limitation is the mind's requirement to have a stable point of reference for the interpretation of incoming information. Without this point of reference, it's impossible to maintain either our ability to reason or our emotional equilibrium. That point of reference is our egoic self.

We tend to take this self for granted, even to malign it—at least, until we lose it as a point of reference. Just ask anyone who has become mentally disoriented as the result of drugs, disease, injury, or even a spiritual awakening. They'll tell you just how precious it is to have a sense of self that does not shift around unexpectedly or even entirely disappear. Even in transformational work, it's necessary to have a stable point of reference if we want to be able to participate in daily life. Or stay out of a mental ward.

As I mentioned in Chapter 8, the nine types provide us with an ordinary sense of self that's relatively stable in nature. The fact that our enneagram orientation does not change makes it a great asset for daily functioning. It gives us not only a stable perspective with predictable limits, but the motivational energy needed to tackle the limitations of the type. We tackle them not to tear them down, but to understand them better so that we can use them more creatively. So our type is really a great resource for creative living—if only we can figure out how to use its energy for some constructive purpose.

From a cultural perspective, the existence of nine distinctive types of people means that we have nine diverse groups, each with characteristic values, talents, and motivations. This ensures the kind of cultural diversity any large group needs in order to prosper. Each enneagram type makes a unique contribution to the world that no other type could make as effectively.

Imagine what life would be like if we lived in a culture where we only had one type, not nine—it would be pretty monomaniacal! Even if we just left one out, it would be a problem. If we eliminated the Ones, there would be no one crusading for justice, making laws, or reminding us of "what is right"! If we ignored the Twos, we'd never get to know our next-door neighbors. If we fired the Threes, the economy would soon be in ruin. If we abandoned the Fours, we'd lose our passion for authenticity (not to mention a whole lot of great art). If we disappeared the Fives—well, don't even think about it, because there go our computer systems and the Internet. If we kicked out the Sixes, who would warn us of potential dangers? And if we spaced out the Sevens, who would make us laugh? Perhaps we could oust the Eights—until we need somebody to step in and take charge of tough problems. So that leaves only the Nines. Surely we could forget about *them*...but then how would we ever find somebody to help us get along with the other eight types?

Well, I guess that we can't really get rid of any of the types. We might like to grouse about the types when they annoy us, but when it comes right down to it, none of them is dispensable—not even our own.

Nine Types, Nine Worlds

The enneagram is like a solar system with nine worlds comprising it, each having its own orbit and character. Together, they form a living system that has the power to stabilize, diversify, and transform.

My aim in this book has been to introduce the enneagram in a way that highlights its dynamism and essentially life-affirming nature. More concretely, it's been to describe the nine types from a positive perspective.

Seeing the type energy as positive isn't the same thing as idealizing the types or denying the fact that each has biases and blind spots. It's more like seeing the glass as half-full instead of half-empty. It's seeing the types (and the ego self) as something of innate value that's designed to support our journey through life.

Our type gives us many gifts. Most of them aren't particularly glamorous or extraordinary. Many are so ordinary that we might not think of them as gifts—things like an eye for detail, the ability to be patient, or the drive to complete the tasks we begin. But these gifts matter. They form the foundation for a grounded life.

The positive enneagram perspective gives us a way to regain our wonder about the ordinary gifts of our type. It's an inclusive approach that's designed to help people realize that ego and Essence are just two ways of looking at the self, not irreconcilable forces in perpetual battle. That battle is *all in our heads!*

We don't need to see ourselves as "a house divided." The geometry of the enneagram doesn't show the types as divided. It shows them as diverse elements within an integral whole.

What is the enneagram, anyway? At its most basic, it's just a circle ringed by nine dots. Each dot is part of the circle. And each has a relationship to every other dot on the circle. When I think of the enneagram in this way, it brings to mind the image of nine children holding hands. Maybe they're enjoying a game like Farmer in the Dell or Ring Around the Rosy. They look happy, because they haven't lost the ability to enjoy simple pleasures.

We've all played such simple games. We've all danced in a circle together. But for most of us, it's a distant memory, because we live in a culture where circle games and dances are mostly abandoned by the age of ten. That's about the point in life when we get drawn into activities that are more organized, high-tech, and expensive.

But we lose something when we leave behind such simple pleasures. We don't notice the loss right away, because we're so eager to grow up. It's only later that it becomes apparent—usually long after we've forgotten how to retrace our steps.

The positive enneagram helps us reconnect with this lost sense of joyfulness and innocence ("inner sense"). This is because it's based on the view that human beings are creative beings that exist within a purposeful cosmos. Our limitations are meant to be a goad to creativity, not an albatross around our necks. They're the means by which we grow.

So our happiness depends less on fixing our faults than on allowing them to transform us. But how can we do this if we hate and fear them? How can we learn from our mistakes if we're afraid to look at them? Or even to risk making them in the first place?

The way out of this dilemma is to give ourselves permission to notice our faults, limitations, and missteps—*but not to dwell on them*. This is a tricky balancing act, because it requires us to be open to self-knowledge but to curb our tendency toward self-judgment. Because as soon as we start to rag on ourselves for having faults, we begin to shut down. Then we can't change anything.

Instead, we can substitute action for self-recrimination. Every time we notice some shortcoming, we can think of how to deal with it in a more positive way. Sometimes this means a change in habits, but it could just mean a change in attitude. It could also mean asking for help via prayer or meditation. Often, taking small but definitive steps works better than making big resolutions that are impossible to fulfill. (A little bit of patience and humor help, as well.)

Positive change is a lifelong project. It can't happen overnight. And it doesn't have a definable outcome: one person's fulfillment is another's dead end, because the path to fulfillment is unique for each of us. Working with the enneagram can help us find the right path for us because it gives us valuable clues about the nature of our energy, motivation, and ways of relating to other people. Enneagram work is most powerful when we use it to develop our potential instead of belaboring our limitations.

Think of children. They have lots of limitations—they're ignorant, unruly, and impatient. But when we look at a small child, is that the main thing we see? No. What we see is their potential. We focus on that potential and how we can develop it. But we also love them for who they are already, despite their naughty ways and limited understanding.

Why not apply the same logic to ourselves? What do we have to lose? With the enneagram, we've got a powerful tool to help us break through some of the tougher barriers to self-understanding. That understanding can go a long ways toward helping us make a breakthrough in our ability to reshape ourselves and our relationships with other people.

When this breakthrough happens, we'll find ourselves in a familiar place: in that circle we knew as small children, the circle of life. There we'll find companions with whom to join hands and celebrate. Together, we'll rediscover what makes life worth living: our ability to laugh, to dance, and to sing.

Appendixes

Appendix A

What's My Type?
(Test I)

Instructions:

Take a look at the nine character profiles on the next page. Each passage describes one of the nine enneagram types.

You can use this test to begin the process of determining your type. It's often easy to immediately cross out two or three descriptions that don't sound at all like you. Of the remaining descriptions, see whether there are any that you're pretty sure don't apply; a realistic goal is to narrow the choices to three or four. (With descriptions this short, it's unlikely that you'll be able to immediately pinpoint your type, but you should at least be able to narrow the field.)

Try combining these results with those of Test II (see Appendix B) and then reading the type descriptions in the book to gain additional insights. If you still have questions about your type, try to attend an enneagram workshop featuring type panels (nine panels grouped by type) to get a visceral sense of the energy that goes with each type.

The *answer key* is upside-down on the page after the paragraphs.

a. I take a careful approach with everything I do. It's important to me to take the time to "do things right" in my work and my life. I enjoy neatness and order. Although it's hard to admit, carelessness or cutting corners—even in little ways—can really bother me. When I see other people doing it, it's hard not to say anything. I try to keep my thoughts to myself, but this can make me tense. There are times when I wish I could loosen up a little without feeling like I'm compromising my values.

b. What matters to me is authenticity and the meaning of life. I would rather have a difficult experience that helps me know myself than success without self-insight. More than other people, I feel a longing for something that is missing. At the same time, I have ways to translate my longing into some form of creative expression via the arts, writing, or just by doing everyday things in an unusual or artistic way. When I'm being creative, I feel like I'm connecting to that part of life that's missing.

c. I'm a matter-of-fact person. I enjoy the little things in life and get along well with most people, so I have a variety of friends. I do find that a regular schedule helps me stay focused and get things done. Otherwise, it's easy to get distracted and lose track of time. Then I can get behind, and it's hard to get caught up. I like to stay calm and avoid conflicts, so I try to help the people around me get along. Personal decisions can be hard for me, so getting ideas from friends can help me decide what to do.

d. What I really care about are people. I enjoy relationships so much—they make my life worthwhile. I would almost always choose to spend time with friends or family than to spend time alone. When I have a special relationship with someone, I put them first in my life. I feel most alive when serving the needs of others and I also like to connect up people that I think might enjoy one another. But I have to be careful not to "over-give," because then I feel burned out and unappreciated.

e. I'm very direct. I speak plainly: I say what I mean and mean what I say. Some people don't like that kind of directness, but that's just how I am. I'm a good friend to the people I trust—I'm always there to help them out of a jam. I look out for my people, even when it costs me. And it *does* cost me at times, because I tend to act first and ask questions later. I've got a temper that can be hard to control. But inside, I'm a marshmallow. You just have to know me well to find that out.

f. I'm exceptionally alert and observant, especially in unfamiliar or public settings. I can spot danger a mile away; I have almost a sixth sense for it. But I can also overreact at times, getting anxious, over-vigilant, or even paranoid. But a watchful disposition does has advantages. I'm a natural skeptic, so I don't get fooled easily. I'm very protective of those I care for, and I have a feisty side when it comes to sticking up for the underdog. Also, I'm extremely loyal to groups I belong to or causes I believe in.

g. Rational thinking and logic make more sense to me than emotional outbursts. When I have a problem, instead of worrying about it, I spend time thinking about it from different angles. So I often come up with an ingenious solution that no one else has thought of. I value relationships but I would usually rather show it in private than in public. I'm a shy person who needs private space and time alone to gather my thoughts. I also use that time to re-charge my batteries, because being with other people takes a lot of energy.

h. What motivates me most in life is personal achievement. I love a challenge—working hard, being the best at what I do, and getting the job done, whatever the obstacles. I'm great at multi-tasking. I can do a lot of things at the same time without losing track of my goals. But sometimes I can get so single-minded about my work that I may lose track of other things that are important, like relationships or recreation. It's possible for me to identify so completely with what I do that I'm not sure who I am apart from my work.

i. Life is such an adventure! It's filled with so many possibilities—and I want to explore as many of them as possible. I'm a high-energy optimist who likes making work into play; my biggest challenge is finding time to do all the things that attract my attention. I have lots of interests and ideas, but I tend to get involved in so many projects that I find myself juggling all the time in order to keep them all afloat. Sometimes this works and sometimes it doesn't. But I'd rather juggle than risk the prospect of getting bored.

Key to Test I:

a. Type 1   b. Type 4   c. Type 9   d. Type 2   e. Type 8   f. Type 6   g. Type 5   h. Type 3   i. Type 7

Appendix B

What's My Type?
(Test II)

The following test is a paper version of my online test (available at www.enneagramdimensions.net, if you prefer to have MS-Excel tally the results).

Instructions:

There are 180 statements (20 per type). In the **white square** to the right of each statement, please rate how well each statement describes you (see the example in the box below):

- 0 = *not at all*
- 1 = *somewhat*
- 2 = *pretty well*
- 3 = *very well*

When you're finished, add up each column to create page totals. Then turn to the scoring page and follow the instructions there.

1. Emotionally intense situations make me feel really alive.

2. I like to do something new, not the same old thing.

3. I take pride in the way I put people at ease.

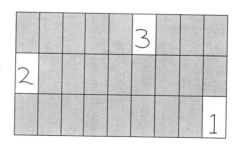

1. I hate asking for help, even though I like giving it.

2. I like the idea of involving my intimate partner in my work life, so we don't drift apart.

3. Most people see me as more peaceful than I really am.

4. I often feel a sense of longing without really knowing why.

5. Having a private space is a necessity, not a luxury.

6. Meeting my deadline matters more than getting every tiny detail just right.

7. My feelings of apprehension are less intense when I have a project to work on.

8. I'm a force to be reckoned with.

9. I can embrace the sweet side of sorrow.

10. My bluntness can sometimes blow people away.

11. My desire to think positive can sometimes be like an addiction.

12. I find it hard to hold back when it comes to offering help and advice.

13. Being a winner makes my efforts worthwhile.

14. Being in nature is deeply soothing to me.

15. I find it hard not to judge people too harshly.

	1	2	3	4	5	6	7	8	9
1									X
2								X	
3				X					
4					X				
5			X						
6							X		
7		X							
8		X							
9					X				
10			X						
11	X								
12							X		
13						X			
14				X					
15						X			

Questions 1-15 TOTAL

16. Making other people laugh helps me feel calmer and less anxious.

17. Emotionally intense situations make me feel really alive.

18. I like to do something new, not the same old thing.

19. I take pride in the way I put people at ease.

20. I like to do so many things that it's easy to spread myself too thin.

21. My desire to achieve knows no bounds.

22. Even when I seem accepted by a group, it's hard to feel that I really belong.

23. I can be stubborn in a way that avoids direct confrontation.

24. People say I have a powerful aura.

25. It's hard not to cry when I feel sentimental, even when I'm in public.

26. I can both make the rules and enforce them.

27. I can feel irritated for no special reason.

28. I am able to create harmony in my environment.

29. I look out for people who can't look out for themselves.

30. Finding my purpose in life means everything to me.

Questions 16-30 TOTAL

31. Maintaining close ties with friends and family helps me feel safe in a chaotic world.

32. I find it hard to bear those aspects of life that dull the heart and kill the soul.

33. I can't help but see both sides of almost any question.

34. I find it unnerving to talk with people who don't seem emotionally engaged.

35. I like to keep life simple and uncomplicated.

36. I prefer to thoroughly think through a problem before I act.

37. Although I can easily imagine panicking in a crisis, in a real emergency, I do surprisingly well.

38. I'm so much more of a heart person than a head person.

39. Getting the job done right is more important than getting the job done fast.

40. I like to read up in advance before trying some new activity.

41. Faith and trust are hard for me, because I doubt things that most people seem to take for granted.

42. Conforming to group norms doesn't allow me to express who I really am.

43. Learning to assert myself gives me confidence and lessens my anxiety.

44. There's nothing I enjoy like making introductions and helping people get to know one another.

45. As a child, I was more serious and realistic than many other children.

Questions 31-45 TOTAL

46. I tend to get myself so heavily scheduled with work that there's not much time to simply sit and reflect.

47. No one's more critical of me than I am of myself.

48. I find it hard to accomplish something without getting distracted.

49. I value originality more than success.

50. My attention too easily goes to worst-case scenarios, even when they are not likely to happen.

51. Details of my childhood sometimes seem hazy and far away.

52. I'm sometimes seen by others as socially unresponsive.

53. I feel an urge to escape when I land in situations that require an emotional commitment.

54. I tend to either respect or defy authority.

55. I like to concentrate on exactly one thing at a time and do not appreciate distractions.

56. I'm optimistic about most things.

57. I'm always aware of the rules I'm supposed to follow, whether I choose to conform to them or break them.

58. I can't imagine life without my many acquaintances and social contacts.

59. Sometimes it's hard to tell the difference between the image I project and the person I am inside.

60. It's hard not to feel nervous when meeting new people.

Questions 46-60 TOTAL

61. My first instinct is always to help people, whether or not they ask for it.

62. In a group situation, I usually prefer to blend in, rather than take the lead or voice objections.

63. People see me as a natural leader.

64. Often I feel that my personal opinions aren't all that essential to a group discussion.

65. I don't have to prove anything to anybody.

66. As a parent or guardian, I'm more strict than permissive.

67. I work hard to succeed because failure is just not an option.

68. I'm more willing than a lot of people to do the "grunt" work on a group project.

69. Being authentic matters more to me than material success.

70. I've got so many ideas buzzing around in my head that it can be hard to work on just one at a time.

71. Controlling my temper is tough.

72. Having daily routines helps me stay on track and get things done.

73. Making a good impression is important to me.

74. Pride is both my greatest strength and my greatest weakness.

75. Making time for relationships can be hard because of my busy schedule.

Questions 61-75 TOTAL

76. Giving, caring, and sharing mean a lot to me.

77. Impartial listening comes easily to me.

78. Ideas often come to me like lightning flashes.

79. I have a lot of nervous energy and an overactive imagination.

80. Emotional insincerity really bothers me.

81. I can get very wrapped up in my concern for others.

82. I have the strength to take on tasks that would defeat a weaker person.

83. My deep emotions are my greatest creative resource.

84. It's unacceptably humiliating to be publicly criticized.

85. People who don't take things seriously annoy me.

86. Nothing motivates me like high achievement.

87. I'm a particularly reliable, loyal, and steady employee.

88. I've been called a perfectionist, although I don't feel very perfect.

89. Because I do so much for others, I sometimes feel entitled to special treatment.

90. Public recognition means a lot to me.

Questions 76-90 TOTAL

91. I tend to see other people as equals.

92. I want to be certain that I'm meeting my own high standards for conduct.

93. When I resonate with someone, it's not on a superficial level.

94. It's important for me to be a sympathetic listener and supportive friend.

95. I appreciate good food, good company, and the good life.

96. Sometimes going on the offense is the only way to conquer fear.

97. I'm strongly drawn to humanitarian work with people or animals.

98. My natural exuberance usually keeps me from getting bogged down in heavy emotions.

99. When I walk in a room full of people, I immediately sense who's in charge.

100. I generally enjoy puttering around and losing myself in the small tasks of ordinary life.

101. I am a careful observer of people and situations.

102. Although I long to be accepted, I hate the idea of mindless conformity.

103. When I care about people, I want to improve their behavior.

104. It's just not that much fun to do only one activity at a time.

105. I'm a natural nurturer.

Questions 91-105 TOTAL

106. I enjoy puzzling out ingenious solutions to unusual problems.

107. I take things personally and don't care who knows it.

108. I find public displays of emotion unappealing.

109. Most people see me as non-judgmental and easy-going.

110. Upholding ethical values and principles is extremely important to me.

111. Translating my inner vision into a work of art can be incredibly compelling.

112. I can adapt my dress and behavior to the needs of the situation.

113. I try to keep my options open.

114. I can ignore painful emotions to get the job done.

115. Games can fascinate me too much.

116. Being in an environment that's plastic and impersonal just drains the life right out of me.

117. I like to study intricate patterns and complex concepts.

118. Sometimes it's hard to get around to my own personal needs.

119. I have a very active inner critic.

120. I can get cranky when things get too complex.

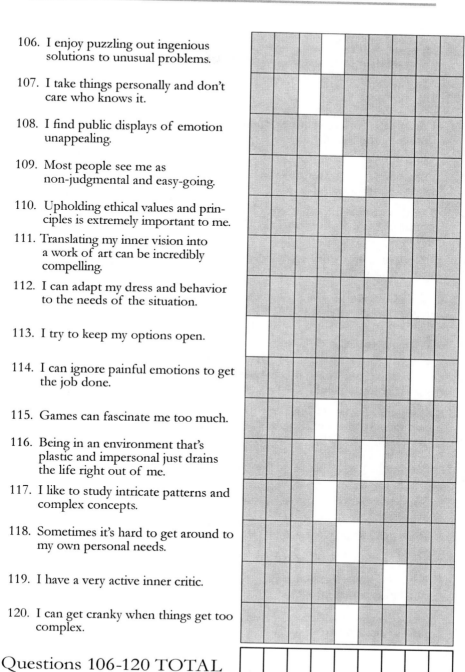

Questions 106-120 TOTAL

121. My home and family provide me with a safe haven in an unsafe world.

122. My word is my bond.

123. I don't care for interruptions when I'm trying to think through a problem.

124. I don't mind giving "tough love" when it's needed.

125. I tend to mentally tune out when people push for an emotional reaction.

126. I feel quite guilty when I get angry without justification.

127. When I like art, it's often something quirky or unusual.

128. Tolerance comes easily to me.

129. I seldom embrace ideas that haven't stood the test of time.

130. Sometimes it takes time for my emotions to catch up with my thoughts.

131. I'm the chief in my circle of friends.

132. Familiar comforts bring me a sense of peace.

133. Feeling vulnerable makes me squirm.

134. Friends describe me as warm, romantic, and affectionate.

135. More than anything, I'm a "can do" kind of person.

Questions 121-135 TOTAL

136. Friends sometimes tell me I'm too hard on myself.

137. It's not hard to be discreet when necessary.

138. I become tense or critical more easily than most people.

139. Being in the public eye is something I generally enjoy.

140. I always protect what's mine.

141. It's my nature to seek novelty, not routine.

142. I'm very sensitive to the moods of other people.

143. Whatever I do, I always try to exceed my personal best.

144. When I get grounded, it helps me carry out existing plans instead of just developing new ones.

145. I'm a systematic thinker who can separate thought from emotion.

146. I'm a natural survivor, and I have the supplies stockpiled to prove it!

147. I can often pick ideas "out of the air."

148. I'm very loyal to people who have earned my trust.

149. I know how it feels to experience intense loneliness.

150. In intimate relationships, I often experience jealous feelings, even though I don't approve of them.

Questions 136-150 TOTAL

151. Achievement and recognition let me know I'm targeting my goals.

152. I'm good at making people laugh, because I have a quick wit and don't take myself too seriously.

153. I value intellectual exchange more than emotional sharing.

154. I use my "inner radar" to intuit the motives of others and decide whether or not it's safe to trust them.

155. I get jazzed about innovative projects or visionary ideas.

156. The words "should" and "ought" crop up a lot in my thinking.

157. Many people find me too emotionally intense or dramatic.

158. I often become an expert on the topics I study.

159. Being alone allows me to get in touch with my innermost self.

160. I'm more detached than emotional.

161. I'm willing to sacrifice in order to be in relationship.

162. I have big appetites and "larger than life" desires.

163. The term "Type A personality" was coined with me in mind.

164. If I walk into a group that lacks a leader, I'll take charge.

165. Sometimes I feel like I'm just going to explode.

Questions 151-165 TOTAL

166. I can be a feisty scrapper who sticks up for the underdog.

167. Small talk doesn't do much for me.

168. Knowing I'm correct takes the edge off the tension I feel.

169. Spending time away from work makes me antsy.

170. I'm naturally playful, fun-loving, and free-spirited.

171. Personal decision making can paralyze me.

172. Feeling appreciated means so much to me.

173. It's sometimes easier to directly confront my fears than allow my imagination to run wild.

174. I'm a great team player.

175. I mentally zone out when I lack time alone.

176. My mind is quick, but not particularly thorough.

177. It's easy to let my friends decide how we spend our time together.

178. I easily identify with the wounds I've received in life.

179. I take action when other people are still trying to sort out their feelings.

180. Freedom matters more to me than almost anything else.

Questions 166-180 TOTAL

TYPE TEST SCORING

1. Transfer the totals for each page to the grid below.

2. Add up each column & place the totals in the boxes at the bottom.

3. Transfer the totals below to the identical positions on the enneagram on the following page. This will show you the scores for each type.

SUBTOTALS:

QUESTIONS 1-15								
QUESTIONS 16-30								
QUESTIONS 31-45								
QUESTIONS 46-60								
QUESTIONS 61-75								
QUESTIONS 76-90								
QUESTIONS 91-105								
QUESTIONS 106-120								
QUESTIONS 121-135								
QUESTIONS 136-150								
QUESTIONS 151-165								
QUESTIONS 166-180								

TOTALS

The highest possible score for any point of view is 60. So the following chart should give you a general idea of how to interpret your results.

> *45 - 60 = Strong indicator for type*
> *30 - 44 = Possible indicator for type*
> *15 - 29 = Weak indicator for type*
> *0 - 14 = Very weak indicator for type*

Please remember that an enneagram typing test is not a definitive tool for determining your type. It's a **support** tool. Only you can determine your type!

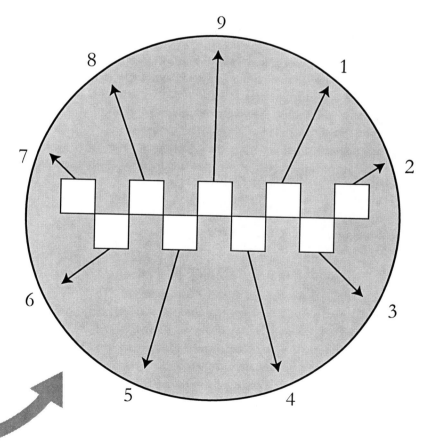

See next page for statements grouped by type >>>>>>

TYPE 1

15   I find it hard not to judge people too harshly.

27   I can feel irritated for no special reason.

39   Getting the job done right is more important than getting the job done fast.

45   As a child, I was more serious and realistic than many other children.

47   No one's more critical of me than I am of myself.

55   I like to concentrate on exactly one thing at a time and do not appreciate distractions.

66   As a parent or guardian, I'm more strict than permissive.

85   People who don't take things seriously annoy me.

88   I've been called a perfectionist, although I don't feel very perfect.

92   I want to be certain that I'm meeting my own high standards for conduct.

103   When I care about people, I want to improve their behavior.

110   Upholding ethical values and principles is extremely important to me.

119   I have a very active inner critic.

126   I feel quite guilty when I get angry without justification.

136   Friends sometimes tell me I'm too hard on myself.

138   I become tense or critical more easily than most people.

150   In intimate relationships, I often experience jealous feelings, even though I don't approve of them.

156   The words "should" and "ought" crop up a lot in my thinking.

165   Sometimes I feel like I'm just going to explode.

168   Knowing I'm correct takes the edge off the tension I feel.

TYPE 2

1   I hate asking for help, even though I like giving it.

12   I find it hard to hold back when it comes to offering help and advice.

19   I take pride in the way I put people at ease.

25   It's hard not to cry when I feel sentimental, even when I'm in public.

34   I find it unnerving to talk with people who don't seem emotionally engaged.

38   I'm so much more of a heart person than a head person.

44   There's nothing I enjoy like making introductions and helping people get to know one another.

58   I can't imagine life without my many acquaintances and social contacts.

61   My first instinct is always to help people, whether or not they ask for it.

74   Pride is both my greatest strength and my greatest weakness.

76	Giving, caring, and sharing mean a lot to me.
81	I can get very wrapped up in my concern for others.
84	It's unacceptably humiliating to be publicly criticized.
89	Because I do so much for others, I sometimes feel entitled to special treatment.
94	It's important for me to be a sympathetic listener and supportive friend.
97	I'm strongly drawn to humanitarian work with people or animals.
105	I'm a natural nurturer.
134	Friends describe me as warm, romantic, and affectionate.
161	I'm willing to sacrifice in order to be in relationship.
172	Feeling appreciated means so much to me.

TYPE 3

2	I like the idea of involving my intimate partners in my work life, so we don't drift apart.
6	Meeting my deadline matters more than getting every tiny detail just right.
13	Being a winner makes my efforts worthwhile.
21	My desire to achieve knows no bounds.
46	I tend to get myself so heavily scheduled with work that there's not much time to simply sit and reflect.
59	Sometimes it's hard to tell the difference between the image I project and the person I am inside.
67	I work hard to succeed because failure is just not an option.
73	Making a good impression is important to me.
75	Making time for relationships can be hard because of my busy schedule.
86	Nothing motivates me like high achievement.
90	Public recognition means a lot to me.
112	I can adapt my dress and behavior to the needs of the situation.
114	I can ignore painful emotions to get the job done.
135	More than anything, I'm a "can do" kind of person.
139	Being in the public eye is something I generally enjoy.
143	Whatever I do, I always try to exceed my personal best.
151	Achievement and recognition let me know I'm targeting my goals.
163	The term "Type A personality" was coined with me in mind.
169	Spending time away from work makes me antsy.
174	I'm a great team player.

TYPE 4

4   I often feel a sense of longing without really knowing why.

9   I can embrace the sweet side of sorrow.

17   Emotionally intense situations make me feel really alive.

22   Even when I seem accepted by a group, it's hard to feel that I really belong.

30   Finding my purpose in life means everything to me.

32   I find it hard to bear those aspects of life that dull the heart and kill the soul.

42   Conforming to group norms doesn't allow me express who I really am.

49   I value originality more than success.

69   Being authentic matters more to me than material success.

80   Emotional insincerity really bothers me.

83   My deep emotions are my greatest creative resource.

93   When I resonate with someone, it's not on a superficial level.

102   Although I long to be accepted, I hate the idea of mindless conformity.

111   Translating my inner vision into a work of art can be incredibly compelling.

116   Being in an environment that's plastic and impersonal just drains the life right out of me.

142   I'm very sensitive to the moods of other people.

149   I know how it feels to experience intense loneliness.

157   Many people find me too emotionally intense or dramatic.

159   Being alone allows me to get in touch with my innermost self.

178   I easily identify with the wounds I've received in life.

TYPE 5

5   Having a private space is a necessity, not a luxury.

36   I prefer to thoroughly think through a problem before I act.

40   I like to read up in advance before trying some new activity.

52   I'm sometimes seen by others as socially unresponsive.

101   I am a careful observer of people and situations.

106   I enjoy puzzling out ingenious solutions to unusual problems.

108   I find public displays of emotion unappealing.

115   Games can fascinate me too much.

117   I like to study intricate patterns and complex concepts.

123   I don't care for interruptions when I'm trying to think through a problem.

125   I tend to mentally tune out when people push for an emotional reaction.

127   When I like art, it's often something quirky or unusual.

130	Sometimes it takes time for my emotions to catch up with my thoughts.
137	It's not hard to be discreet when necessary.
145	I'm a systematic thinker who can separate thought from emotion.
153	I value intellectual exchange more than emotional sharing.
158	I often become an expert on the topics I study.
160	I'm more detached than emotional.
167	Small talk doesn't do much for me.
175	I mentally zone out when I lack time alone.

TYPE 6

7	My feelings of apprehension are less intense when I have a project to work on.
16	Making other people laugh helps me feel calmer and less anxious.
31	Maintaining close ties with friends and family helps me feel safe in a chaotic world.
37	Although I can easily imagine panicking in a crisis, in a real emergency, I do surprisingly well.
41	Faith and trust are hard for me, because I doubt things that most people seem to take for granted.
43	Learning to assert myself gives me confidence and lessens my anxiety.
50	My attention too easily goes to worst-case scenarios, even when they are not likely to happen.
54	I tend to either respect or defy authority.
57	I'm always aware of the rules I'm supposed to follow, whether I choose to conform to them or break them.
60	It's hard not to feel nervous when meeting new people.
68	I'm more willing than a lot of people to do the "grunt" work on a group project.
79	I have a lot of nervous energy and an overactive imagination.
87	I'm a particularly reliable, loyal, and steady employee.
96	Sometimes going on the offense is the only way to conquer fear.
121	My home and family provide me with a safe haven in an unsafe world.
129	I seldom embrace ideas that haven't stood the test of time.
148	I'm very loyal to people who have earned my trust.
154	I use my "inner radar" to intuit the motives of others and decide whether or not it's safe to trust them.
166	I can be a feisty scrapper who sticks up for the underdog.
173	It's sometimes easier to directly confront my fears than allow my imagination to run wild.

TYPE 7

11   My desire to think positive can sometimes be like an addiction.

18   I like to do something new, not the same old thing.

20   I like to do so many things that it's easy to spread myself too thin.

53   I feel an urge to escape when I land in situations that require an emotional commitment.

56   I'm optimistic about most things.

70   I've got so many ideas buzzing around in my head that it can be hard to work on just one at a time.

78   Ideas often come to me like lightning flashes.

91   I tend to see other people as equals.

95   I appreciate good food, good company, and the good life.

98   My natural exuberance usually keeps me from getting bogged down in heavy emotions.

104   It's just not that much fun to do only one activity at a time.

113   I try to keep my options open.

141   It's my nature to seek novelty, not routine.

144   When I get grounded, it helps me carry out existing plans instead of just developing new ones.

147   I can often pick ideas "out of the air."

152   I'm good at making people laugh, because I have a quick wit and don't take myself too seriously.

155   I get jazzed about innovative projects or visionary ideas.

170   I'm naturally playful, fun-loving, and free-spirited.

176   My mind is quick, but not particularly thorough.

180   Freedom matters more to me than almost anything else.

TYPE 8

8   I'm a force to be reckoned with.

10   My bluntness can sometimes blow people away.

24   People say I have a powerful aura.

26   I can both make the rules and enforce them.

29   I look out for people who can't look out for themselves.

63   People see me as a natural leader.

65   I don't have to prove anything to anybody.

71   Controlling my temper is tough.

82   I have the strength to take on tasks that would defeat a weaker person.

99   When I walk in a room full of people, I immediately sense who's in charge.

107   I take things personally and don't care who knows it.

122   My word is my bond.

124   I don't mind giving "tough love" when it's needed.

131   I'm the chief in my circle of friends.

133   Feeling vulnerable makes me squirm.

140   I always protect what's mine.

146   I'm a natural survivor, and I have the supplies stockpiled to prove it!

162   I have big appetites and "larger than life" desires.

164   If I walk into a group that lacks a leader, I'll take charge.

179   I take action when other people are still trying to sort out their feelings.

TYPE 9

3   Most people see me as more peaceful than I really am.

14   Being in nature is deeply soothing to me.

23   I can be stubborn in a way that avoids direct confrontation.

28   I am able to create harmony in my environment.

33   I can't help but see both sides of almost any question.

35   I like to keep life simple and uncomplicated.

48   I find it hard to accomplish something without getting distracted.

51   Details of my childhood sometimes seem hazy and far away.

62   In a group situation, I usually prefer to blend in, rather than take the lead or voice objections.

64   Often I feel that my personal opinions aren't all that essential to a group discussion.

72   Having daily routines helps me stay on track and get things done.

77   Impartial listening comes easily to me.

100   I generally enjoy puttering around and losing myself in the small tasks of ordinary life.

109   Most people see me as non-judgmental and easy-going.

118   Sometimes it's hard to get around to my own personal needs.

120   I can get cranky when things get too complex.

128   Tolerance comes easily to me.

132   Familiar comforts bring me a sense of peace.

171   Personal decision making can paralyze me.

177   It's easy to let my friends decide how we spend our time together.

Appendix C

What's My Subtype?*

Instructions:

There are 36 statements, each with three possible responses. For each response, fill in the **white square** with a rating indicating how well each response describes you (see example in the box below):

- *0 = not at all*
- *1 = somewhat*
- *2 = pretty well*
- *3 = very well*

HINT: LOOK AT ALL THREE RESPONSES BEFORE RATING EACH ONE.

When you're finished, add up each column to create page totals. Then turn to the scoring page and follow the instructions there.

---

1. When I want to relax I like to
   a. get out in nature
   b. eat a delicious meal
   c. take a nap

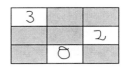

---

*Although I designed this test, I received extensive input on the content from my friend and enneagram colleague, Dina Innominato. Thanks, Dina!

1. In daily life, I seek out
    a. opportunities to do creative work
    b. projects that need my support
    c. ways to make my house a home

2. I particularly hope to
    a. share my life with someone special
    b. live responsibly
    c. make an impact on the world

3. My metaphorical self can be described as
    a. a fiery furnace of burning passion
    b. a small but potent seed
    c. an intelligent self-organizing system

4. When I travel, I take things that
    a. make me feel at home
    b. make a great impression
    c. make for an interesting journey

5. I focus a lot on
    a. the practical side of life
    b. ways to make life exciting
    c. organized activities

6. When it comes to peace, I tend to be a
    a. peace seeker
    b. peace breaker
    c. peace maker

Questions 1 - 6 TOTAL

7. At a party, I look for
   a. a stranger who looks interesting
   b. opportunities to make contacts
   c. people I know

8. I take particular satisfaction in
   a. helping people get organized
   b. fulfilling my personal commitments
   c. making my partner feel special

9. I'm irritated by people who are
   a. boring
   b. embarrassing
   c. unreliable

10. If I were a body in space, I'd be
    a. the earth
    b. the solar system
    c. a shooting star

11. I identify with the expression
    a. "Follow your passion."
    b. "I'm okay, you're okay."
    c. "There's no place like home."

12. My "inner child" shows up in my tendency to
    a. act out & push the limits
    b. seek approval for good behavior
    c. indulge myself with personal treats

Questions 7 - 12 TOTAL

13. More than other people, I
    a. make my own way in life
    b. risk my life for peak experiences
    c. tune into current events & trends

14. I particularly appreciate
    a. time alone
    b. satisfying community work
    c. intense stimulation

15. Spiritually, I seek out
    a. a sense of contentment
    b. universal communion
    c. ecstatic union

16. If I were a book, I'd be
    a. a love story
    b. a down-to-earth "how-to" guide
    c. a book on social or political trends

17. I especially value the way I relate to
    a. my community
    b. my soul mate
    c. myself

18. I like a workplace environment that
    a. facilitates team building
    b. allows me to get something done
    c. gets my creative juices flowing

Questions 13 - 18 TOTAL

19. I see my life partner as
    a.   someone with shared goals
    b.   my best friend
    c.   the wellspring of my very existence

20. I'd like to be admired for my
    a.   organizing ability and social vision
    b.   creativity and originality
    c.   decency and work ethic

21. I'm extremely productive when working
    a.   on my own
    b.   with the right people
    c.   with one stimulating partner

22. I'd find it very hard to sacrifice
    a.   my autonomy
    b.   my primary relationship
    c.   my contacts

23. When I dress, I look for clothes that are
    a.   appropriate for the situation
    b.   easy to care for
    c.   self-expressive

24. My friends particularly appreciate my
    a.   artistic flair
    b.   dependability
    c.   good taste

Questions 19 - 24 TOTAL

25. When I walk into a room full of people, I'm sure to notice
    a. opportunities to network
    b. the comfortability of the room
    c. possibilities for intimacy

26. At times I can be
    a. too conforming
    b. too ungrounded
    c. too unadventurous

27. If I wanted to sell food, I'd establish
    a. an intimate little bistro
    b. a well-run catering company
    c. a grocery store or neighborhood cafe

28. When I make friends, I tend to
    a. share confidences with them
    b. look for activities to do with them
    c. find practical ways to support them

29. I like the work I do to reflect my
    a. creativity and talent
    b. personal commitment to quality
    c. social or political concerns

30. I'm especially uncomfortable
    a. at big gatherings
    b. being chained to a desk
    c. spending time alone

Questions 25 - 30 TOTAL

31. The way I speak tends to be

    a. spontaneous

    b. diplomatic

    c. direct

32. My idea of home is

    a. a place to call my own

    b. a place to regroup

    c. a place to experience intimacy

33. Others probably see me as

    a. more imaginative than boring

    b. more serious than frivolous

    c. more concerned than apathetic

34. If I were a bird, I would resemble

    a. an industrious robin

    b. a dignified swan

    c. a crazy cockatoo

35. I'm at my best when dealing with

    a. the new & unusual

    b. the responsibilities of life

    c. socially complex situations

36. I tend to be preoccupied with

    a. social involvement or reform

    b. intensity seeking

    c. security issues

Questions 31 - 36 TOTAL

SUBTYPES TEST SCORING

Questions 1 - 6 TOTAL

Questions 7 - 12 TOTAL

Questions 13 - 18 TOTAL

Questions 19 - 24 TOTAL

Questions 25 - 30 TOTAL

Questions 31 - 36 TOTAL

GRAND TOTAL

⇩   ⇩   ⇩

Self-preservation subtype

Sexual subtype

Social subtype

Interpreting Your Score:

A score of 0 – 108 is possible for each subtype arena. An average score would be 54, so a score of 65 or more indicates a strong emphasis for that subtype arena; a score over 80 indicates a very strong emphasis.

Please note: The score on this subtypes test depends in part on what is happening in your life at the time you are taking the test. A big shock might move you towards a self-preservation orientation while a sudden windfall might result in higher scores for the sexual or social arenas. So while your subtype emphasis is relatively stable, the scores can shift somewhat depending on your life circumstances.

For more info....

On how to order *The Positive Enneagram*:
Order online from Amazon.com, from your local bookstore through Lightning Source (Ingram), or from the author's web site: www.enneagramdimensions.net.

On quantity discounts or international orders:
Contact the author at geraniumpress@gmail.com.

On the positive enneagram approach:
Visit Enneagram Dimensions (www.enneagramdimensions. net) for more information, including articles on many enneagram-related topics. You might also consider subscribing to the *Enneagram Monthly* (www.ennea.org), where Susan Rhodes is the staff writer.

Want to share your thoughts on *The Positive Enneagram*?
Please consider writing a book review for Amazon.com. This is a great way to start a discussion about the ideas presented here. (To create a review, go to the *Positive Enneagram* page on Amazon, scroll down to Customer Reviews and click on the CREATE YOUR OWN REVIEW button on the right.)

LaVergne, TN USA
12 November 2010
204486LV00008B/3/P